UTAH BEACH 6 JUNE 1944 THE D-DAY LANDING

Please enjoy!

ROBERT J. PARKER

AMBERLEY

Acknowledgements

I would like to offer thanks to Jonathan Reeve and Jonathan Jackson for their enthusiasm in suggesting this project from the earliest stage, and to all of the editorial staff at Amberley Publishing for their energy and effort in completing this volume. That would surely include Connor Stait, Louis Archard, Patricia Curley, and Vicki Fletcher, along with the entire production team. Most importantly, I would dearly love to thank my wife Sheila for her support and patience in the writing of this D-Day series. Any and all errors of fact or interpretation are entirely mine.

RJP
Valparaiso, Indiana

About the Author

Robert J. Parker holds Bachelors and Masters degrees in history. He currently lectures in US history at Purdue University Northwest and has written several books concerning British and American history, including Amberley's *Passchendaele 1917* and *British Prime Ministers*. He resides in Valparaiso, Indiana, just outside of Chicago, and visits the United Kingdom regularly. He travels extensively and has visited over eighty countries on six continents.

First published 2019

Amberley Publishing
The Hill, Stroud
Gloucestershire, GL5 4EP

www.amberley-books.com

British Library Cataloguing in Publication Data.
A catalogue record for this book is available from the British Library.

ISBN 978 1 4456 6928 1 (paperback)
ISBN 978 1 4456 6929 8 (ebook)

Typesetting and Origination by Amberley Publishing.
Printed in Great Britain.

Contents

Chapter 1

Introduction

The history of war does not know of an undertaking comparable to it for breadth of conception, grandeur of scale, and mastery of execution.

Josef Stalin

In the spring of 1943 a plan was being devised for the invasion of north-western Europe by the Allied armed forces. The Combined Chiefs of Staff, British and American, selected British Lieutenant General Fredrick Morgan for the task of designing and coordinating this project. It was to be the long-promised second front: the arrival of the Allied armies, leading to the liberation of France. Morgan and his team then produced the basic plan that would become Operation Overlord, the amphibious crossing of the English Channel to challenge Adolf Hitler's Atlantic Wall.

Up to this point there had been several programs, all with a variety of codenames, and all focused on achieving the same goal: the invasion of Western Europe by the Allies. Since June 1941, when the Soviet Union had been attacked and overrun by Hitler's Nazi onslaught, Soviet leader Josef Stalin had been begging, pleading and cajoling the Allied leaders to open a second front in Western Europe. Stalin, desperate for help in his war of self-preservation, had become frustrated and increasingly skeptical of the repeated promises of a second front made by Britain and the United States. The Soviet Red Army had fought tenaciously to escape complete defeat against the weight of the German Wehrmacht, at times barely, and the need for a second front to counter the German invasion continued. British Prime Minister Winston Churchill and American President Franklin Roosevelt, along with their respective chief military advisors, adopted three basic plans: 'Sledgehammer', 'Bolero' and 'Roundup'. All three were frequently adorned with various coded labels, but in essence it boiled down to three policies to meet three distinct goals.

Sledgehammer would be an emergency invasion of France by a small but relatively unprepared invasion force to immediately relieve pressure on the Russian front. Sledgehammer would hopefully save the Soviets from surrender and defeat, and keep them in the war – an absolutely vital part of Allied strategy for defeating Hitler. Although frequently discussed, no real consideration was ever given to activating Sledgehammer and it was never given much chance for success if it was to be forced into implementation. Often broached as an alternative by the American advisors, it was ardently opposed by the British as too little, too early and utterly doomed if it was ever attempted. Ignoring the fact that there were barely enough resources to carry out such an attempt, there was no definitive thought as to where or how troops would be transported and landed onto the European continent.

Bolero was the continuous buildup and delivery to Britain of men, supplies and equipment in order to conduct a full-scale invasion of Western Europe at some point in the near future. It relied on the tremendous industrial output of the United States, which while simultaneously fighting a far-flung war in the Pacific against the Empire of Japan, was still possessed of a colossal capacity to produce the mountains of material required to conduct the invasion of France. Bolero also hinged on the Allies' ability to successfully blunt the challenge of the German U-boats, which at one time had threatened the very survival of Great Britain by cutting off the island nation from all resupply. Although that threat remained throughout 1943, it had gradually been reduced, allowing tons of food and thousands of tanks, planes, landing craft, weapons and soldiers to be transported along the Atlantic sea lanes to Britain. The magnitude of this progressive buildup, so essential for the invasion, was an accomplishment of logistical brilliance and brawn.

Roundup, along with other related code names, was to be the full-scale invasion and re-conquest of Europe. It eventually assumed the name Operation Overlord, with the actual D-Day landing being named Operation Neptune. Whereas the Americans were all for invading as soon as possible, the British were more hesitant to go up against the acknowledged and admittedly formidable strength of the German forces. To the endless consternation of the United States, and the impatience of Stalin and the Soviet Union, 1943 became dedicated to action in the Mediterranean, Sicily and Italy, while the invasion of France continued to be postponed. Eventually, spring 1944 was chosen, but even then a delay from May until June was required.

'D-Day' was a generic term applied to dozens of decision days, landing days or operation days, whether in the Atlantic or the Pacific theatres, but of course, it has come to mean the 6 June 1944 Normandy invasion. It was this program, under any and all of its various code names and descriptions, that General Morgan and his staff of British and American war chiefs were assigned to plan. Temporarily, and until the actual operational commander was appointed late in 1943, Morgan was the 'designated' Chief of Staff, Supreme Allied Commander (COSSAC). In December 1943, President Roosevelt chose for that prestigious position American General Dwight D. Eisenhower who, with his own group of advisors and generals, would flesh out Morgan's basic invasion plan and craft it into his own vision. Eisenhower worked well with Morgan, even naming him his deputy chief of staff for the invasion. Soon thereafter, Eisenhower appointed his Supreme Headquarters Allied Expeditionary Force (SHAEF) staff, embracing a liberal blend of British and American commanders to oversee all aspects of the military operation. That staff included British General Sir Bernard Montgomery as commander of ground forces for the Overlord invasion.

Morgan originally planned on three landing beaches in Normandy, using three divisions, with two in reserve – a number dictated by arithmetic. The Allies' invasion plans were always predicated on and constrained by numbers: how many transports, how many landing craft and how many men could be immediately delivered, reinforced and resupplied? It was an incredibly complicated logistical puzzle. Because it would have to be an amphibious invasion, every soldier landed required so many tons of 'lift' just to transport him and his equipment onto a beach. A continuous and essential amount of 'lift' would then be required thereafter for all ensuing resupply and replacements onto the captured beach. 'Lift' demanded, at the very least, the minimum amount of material to maintain that landed soldier and allow him to be sufficiently resupplied and reinforced in strength in order to drive inland and off of the beach. There were only so many vessels available for every stage of the operation: minesweepers to prepare lanes of safe passage for every ship to cross the English Channel and anchor near the beaches; warships (large and small) to protect and soften the beach defences in preparation of landing; and landing craft to ferry the soldiers and their equipment to the beaches. Every extra man or piece of equipment meant a prodigious logistical chain of supply that extended all the way back to the factories and farms of the United States.

Once the strength required for all phases of the operation had been calculated, Morgan and his team selected where to land the invasion force. The selected beaches had to have certain qualities in order to better afford and gain the essential foothold. It was conceded by the Allies, but not by the Germans, that attempting to invade and capture a major deep-water port on Day 1 would not be practical or economical as a tactical goal. Therefore, deep-water ports such as Calais, Le Havre and Rotterdam were all eliminated. However, beaches near major ports were proposed with the assumption that a successful landing, followed by a quick strike, could possibly capture an intact deep-water port nearby. Normandy provided many of these attributes. Normandy was close enough to the ports of embarkation to deliver the invasion force and to allow rapid reinforcement and resupply; it was also near enough to provide complete around-the-clock air cover for both the invasion and the following breakout; and it was near to a major French deep-water port, Cherbourg, which could be isolated from German reinforcement by cutting off the neck of the Cotentin Peninsula, giving an invasion force the opportunity to rapidly seize its harbour facilities intact.

A further major consideration was the strength of the German defences. Closer targets, directly across the narrow 30-mile Strait of Dover, such as the Pas de Calais, bristled with heavily fortified defences and nearby German armoured Panzer units. The Calais area would offer a distance advantage, but at a decidedly greater expenditure in casualties and a higher risk of failure. Normandy, although adequately defended, was felt to offer a less costly location in terms of casualties and with a much higher chance of success.

Therefore, Morgan and his staff chose Normandy, and this became the basis for the invasion objectives that were presented to General Eisenhower when he arrived in Britain to assume his post as Chief of Staff, Supreme Allied Commander (COSSAC) in January 1944. Eisenhower was impressed with the plan, as was his ground forces commander, British General Sir Bernard Montgomery. After carefully studying the Overlord plan,

'Monty' recommended an increase in the number of beaches and units to commence the landing operations. Both Montgomery and Eisenhower quickly agreed that three beaches and three divisions for the initial assault were inadequate. A major problem had been the lack of landing craft, but thanks to increased availability, the enlargement of the landing force to five beaches and ten divisions could be accommodated.

Utah Beach was the last beach added to the Operation Overlord menu. It was decided in early 1944 that since the Normandy target would require a broader sweep of invasion territory in order to be successful, a greater number of invading and reinforcing soldiers would be required. Utah Beach would also provide an opportunity to capture the deep-water port of Cherbourg. This prize would immediately provide greater capacity for the monumental logistical necessities: resupply and reinforcement. Located at the northern edge of the Cotentin Peninsula, Utah Beach's close proximity to this important deep-water harbour was among the ultimate deciding factors for adding the Utah Beach sector to the invasion agenda.

Unlike the desperate struggle at the adjacent Omaha Beach, the Utah Beach invasion landing and advance would go smoothly and without significant losses. Utah would also be different in other ways. It would be the largest use of airborne forces by the US Army to that point in the Second World War. In the same way as the British airborne units sought to land behind the British Sword Beach, at the opposite eastern end of the invasion beaches, the US Army would drop nearly 14,000 soldiers by parachute and glider to better secure the entire south-western flank of the invasion area. This massive airborne contingent would seek to deny the Germans any attempts to reinforce against the Allied landing units arriving on the beach. Utah would also accelerate the opportunity to open a path for the rapid choking off of the Cotentin Peninsula and the possibility for an expedient thrust to the north-west and a quick capture of Cherbourg.

Such were the operational plans for Utah Beach as incorporated into the Overlord plan.

'The Big Three' (Stalin, Roosevelt and Churchill) meeting at the Tehran Conference in December 1943. It was here that Roosevelt announced to Stalin the date of the spring 1944 D-Day landing and the name of the supreme commander for Operation Overlord. This encouraged Stalin concerning the Allied commitment, but there would be another six months, and more delays, before execution. (LOC)

Above left: Franklin Roosevelt had been pressing for an Allied invasion of north-west Europe since the American entry into the Second World War in December 1941. (LOC)

Above right: Josef Stalin had also been desperately urging an Allied second front since the German invasion of the Soviet Union in June of 1941. He was increasingly suspicious of Allied reluctance to embark on this enterprise. (LOC)

German Panzer divisions were an enormous threat to the Allied invasion if they could be rapidly brought to bear from their reserve positions. The scattered veteran German units manning Hitler's Atlantic Wall would prove to be a stubborn foe throughout the Normandy campaign, but especially at Omaha Beach on D-Day. (NARA)

By 1944, and the lurking danger of a successful Allied invasion, Adolf Hitler was now seriously confronted by the possibility of a major second Allied front. (NARA)

Above left: Stalin and German Foreign Minister Joachim Ribbentrop agreeing to the infamous Nazi-Soviet Pact in 1939, prior to the start of the Second World War. Hitler then invaded Soviet Russia in June 1941, placing Stalin in the Allied camp and starting a devastating war on the Eastern Front. Hitler now sought to avoid a second front in the west, while Stalin demanded one from Great Britain and America. (LOC)

Above right: The American military cemetery above Omaha Beach at Colleville-sur-Mer today. The Allies suffered a combined total of 10,000 casualties during the D-Day assault, with roughly 4,400 killed. (RJP)

A typical huge 'big gun' battery located along the French coast. The problem for the Germans was what part of the French coast would be invaded to use such weapons; therefore, the entire French coast received fortification. (Bundesarchiv)

Above left: General Frederick Morgan. Morgan had been in charge of the original planning of the strategy, tactics and location for Overlord (COSSAC). When Eisenhower became supreme Overlord commander (SHAEF), he included Morgan as his deputy chief of staff. (NARA)

Above right: Prime Minister Winston Churchill had heroically kept Britain fighting during the early part of the Second World War. He and his lead military advisor, General Sir Alan Brooke, remained gravely concerned about the difficulty and feasibility of an Allied invasion of France. American General Dwight Eisenhower (center) had been made supreme commander for the invasion, a position Brooke had coveted but was denied. (LOC)

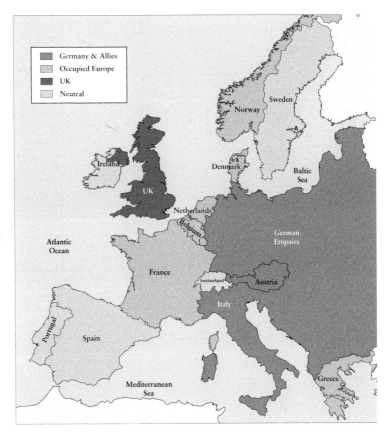

Right: Western Europe during much of the Second World War suffered under Nazi occupation. Britain's island location was essential in preventing German victory.

Below: Many potential invasion routes to liberate Europe were considered. Normandy offered the greatest combination of assets and likelihood of success.

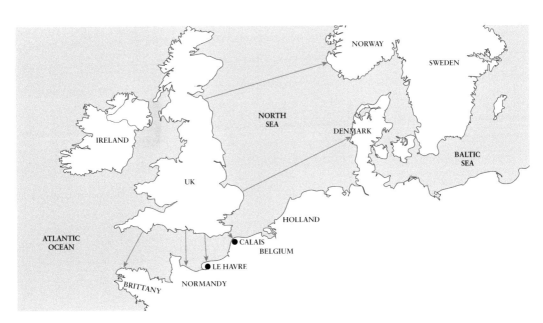

Chapter 2

Why Utah Beach?

I believe we can lick the Hun only by being ahead of him in ideas as well as in material resources.

American Chief of Staff General George Marshall

Utah Beach, on the extreme western end of the Normandy landing site, along with the British Sword Beach at the extreme eastern end, formed the two outer flanking beaches of the expanded programme recommended by the newly appointed Allied high command. The additions were called for after Generals Sir Bernard Montgomery and Dwight Eisenhower agreed on the necessity to have a more potent arrival force right from day one of the invasion. They also concluded that the three-beach approach would be too narrow and congested for follow-up reinforcements to enter, and they feared it would provide the Germans greater opportunity for a more concentrated point of counterattack when attempting to drive the Allies off the beaches and back into the English Channel. Montgomery's first and immediate recommendation on reviewing the Overlord plan was to broaden and increase the invasion site to include five beaches and a total of ten divisions, including reserves. Eisenhower too had reviewed an early rendition of the Overlord plan and had also concluded that the initial landing phase lacked punch. Now, as supreme commander of the invasion force, he readily and enthusiastically concurred with Montgomery and notified his commander, Chief of Staff General George Marshall, of the request. Back in Washington, Marshall gave his approval.

There were other noteworthy considerations to favour the inclusion of Utah Beach. The Americans had enough manpower assembled and in reserve to easily expand their participation; the problem would be having enough transport vessels to cross the English Channel, and landing craft to shuttle them to the beach. This requirement, termed 'lift', would always be a major consideration for any increase in the size of the invading force. Sufficient 'lift' was now available. Since the Utah Beach sector would draw the Allies closer to the Cotentin Peninsula, the potential to quickly seize the large deep-water port of Cherbourg would be increased. Securing a deep-water port was a key component in all planning, due not only to the need to resupply and reinforce the invading force, but also for the far more expeditious arrangement of offloading transports directly upon arrival from across the Atlantic.

Finally, Allied intelligence information had indicated that the area around Utah Beach was only lightly defended. So, coupled with the inclusion of additional breadth for the entire invasion beach area, and having a superior jumping-off point to the upper Cotentin Peninsula, Utah Beach made good tactical and strategic sense and was enthusiastically added to the invasion plans.

The sheer number of American soldiers arriving in Britain was encouraging, but the number of veteran and properly trained units would be limited. This problem was intertwined with the lack of transports and landing craft to accommodate the larger invasion force – always a major dilemma. Plus, additional troops would require the accompanying transport of extra equipment, vehicles and supply – everything from rations to ammunition. More beaches also demanded increased offshore firepower, to pound the beaches in the pre-dawn bombardment, and that meant extra minesweepers and destroyers to clear and protect the additional transports. It was an exponential function. In one area, however, there was no question of availability and superiority: control of the air. Allied airpower was supreme. There, however, the problem was not size or strength, but management and administration. What type and number of planes should be assigned to specific missions, and under whose command would they be placed? For the Overlord operation, it was determined that Eisenhower and his staff would have complete priority. However, there was much bickering and feuding over direct control, numbers and particularly about targets.

The airborne operation would also be a fundamental feature of Utah and Sword, the two beaches securing Overlord's flanks. The British airborne units were assigned to drop in behind the beach on the left flank – Sword Beach. This would secure bridges and junctions and prevent German reserves from reinforcing the defenders at the British and Canadian beaches of Sword, Gold and Juno. The Americans would use their two airborne divisions to solidify their hold on the right flank by doing a pre-dawn drop behind Utah Beach. These two operations ended up with a favourable result on all counts. Unfortunately, the crawl up the Cotentin Peninsula, although successful, was too slow to take Cherbourg intact. The Germans stubbornly defended and then destroyed the port facilities before the Allies could capture them. The entire port had to be totally rehabilitated before any large-scale operations could take place.

Though suffering fairly high casualties (16 per cent), the airborne operation actually incurred fewer casualties than feared (upwards of 70 per cent). Despite the casualties and widespread confusion of the nighttime delivery, the effort by the paratroopers of the American 101st and 82nd airborne divisions was entirely successful in the sense of securing the western flank and protecting the Utah Beach invasion forces soon to be arriving that morning. The move up the Cotentin Peninsula would not be quite so easy or as rapid.

Utah incorporated roughly 11 miles of sandy beach, but unlike Omaha Beach to the east, it was without the surrounding bluffs that provided the German defenders with such a strongly defensible position. Even though driven off course by rough seas on approach, the Utah Beach landings on D-Day were efficiently and effectively carried out with minimum casualties. The securing of the beach, uniting with the

American forces from Omaha Beach and moving up the Cotentin Peninsula were soon underway.

Being the most westerly of the invasion beaches, Utah was pivotal as it would protect the western shoulder of the Normandy invasion. Abutting the junction between the Normandy coast and the Cotentin Peninsula, it was in an area that was rather weakly defended. The city of Cherbourg, however, was heavily garrisoned and fortified against seizure. The question was not whether the city could be captured, but rather if the port could be seized while it remained intact. The goal was to deny the Germans enough time to destroy it, thereby acquiring a functioning facility. Utah Beach would therefore serve as the springboard for cutting off the Cotentin Peninsula and the movement up toward Cherbourg.

Although thinly defended, Utah Beach did not come without some significant disadvantages. The area directly behind it had been intentionally flooded by the Germans, forming a shallow and swampy marsh that would hinder airborne drops and prevent a broad and rapid overrunning of the area by any attempted Allied invasion.

General George Marshall was adamant when it came to Operation Overlord and the need to defeat Germany through north-western Europe. Marshall had aspired to being the Overlord supreme commander, but ceded to FDR's wish for Marshall to remain in Washington, D.C. as his chief advisor and overall military director. Marshall then recommended Eisenhower for leadership of Overlord. Marshall remained FDR's most important military advisor through the course of the Second World War. It was Marshall and Roosevelt who continually pressured Britain for an Allied invasion of France. (US Army)

This presented challenges when it came to advancing from the beach and linking up with scattered airborne elements. Utah Beach would be taken in the first few hours of the landing and secured by noon. Ironically, the confused and unintended scattering of the two airborne divisions all over the southern base of the Cotentin Peninsula ended up working to the Allies' advantage. The Germans were completely confused as to how many paratroopers had been dropped and where they were, since they seemed to be everywhere. Covering so wide an area, the dispersed units also appeared to be much greater in number than they actually were.

The wandering individual troopers, showing amazing persistence and ingenuity, eventually located their comrades and fashioned small groups that would form organized elements of well trained and highly motivated units that operated heroically and effectively. Bridges were blocked, broken or captured; towns and intersections were occupied; and German phone lines were cut. Amid the chaos, sporadic and fierce firefights broke out. These actions began alerting the Germans that the Allies were arriving, but it was not ascertained if it was the main invasion or a diversion in force. By the time the Germans figured it out, it was too late and the Allies were established on Utah Beach.

American Sherman 'wading' tanks being loaded onto landing craft prior to D-Day. These tanks featured air intakes that allowed the vehicles to enter and wade through the low surf and negotiate the invasion beach. (NARA)

A German concrete bunker overlooking the English Channel at Longues-sur-Mer, similar to those near Utah Beach. Shell damage is clearly visible on the upper casement. A few of these bunkers retain their Second World War weapons. This nearly intact battery lies just east of Omaha Beach. (RJP)

US soldiers rehearsing beach landings in Britain prior to D-Day. (LOC)

American soldiers getting ready to board D-Day transports in Weymouth. Several GIs are seen with Bangalore torpedoes over their shoulders. (NARA)

American sailors and soldiers loading equipment onto various transport vessels prior to D-Day. The global war required an enormous capacity to transport tons of equipment, supplies and weapons around the world. (NARA)

Utah Beach was the most westerly of the five assaulted beaches and compared to Omaha Beach the casualties were extremely light – less than 700. However, the airborne assault behind Utah incurred another 2,500. Utah was not plagued by the high surrounding bluffs that enabled German defenders to occupy such a strong defensive position against the Omaha Beach assault. (RJP)

A pair of German 105 mm naval guns used for beach and Channel defense. (RJP)

General Sir Bernard Montgomery had defeated German general Erwin Rommel in North Africa, winning the important battle of El Alamein. He was Eisenhower's first choice to be overall ground commander for Operation Overlord. It was Montgomery and Eisenhower who expanded the three-beach plan developed by Morgan into the five-beach invasion strategy that became Operation Overlord. (NARA)

Chapter 3

Overlord Commanders

General Eisenhower is the captain of the team and I am proud to serve under him …
he is the right man for the job … and in every way an Allied Commander … I would
trust him to the last gasp.

British General Sir Bernard Montgomery

For the Normandy invasion, the chain of command descended cleanly and directly
from President Franklin Roosevelt to General George Marshall and to the person
chosen to be in supreme command of the overall operation, General Dwight D.
Eisenhower. The thread could not have been sharper and more direct. Political leaders
make grand policy and appoint the commanders. Commanders attempt to achieve
in the field the desired results as envisioned by their superiors, the decision makers.
Those commanders entrusted to carry out these great plans rely on skill, organization,
experience and – inevitably – good fortune.

Anxious to seize the offensive and attack and conquer Nazi Germany, Roosevelt
was following his own intuition and his personal assurances to Soviet Russia's leader,
Josef Stalin, that a second front on the continent of Europe would be opened as soon
as possible. Stalin was notorious for frequently and persistently accusing the Western
Allies of reneging on their commitment to the second front, if not in word of promise,
then in speed of delivery. Fearing another Dunkirk disaster, British Prime Minister
Winston Churchill and his commanders were in no hurry to launch a premature attack
on the Germans with an invasion of France. Although Roosevelt was eager to engage
the American army against the Germans somewhere, Stalin deemed the operations
in North Africa, Sicily and Italy to be 'sideshows'. Churchill and his generals feared
and respected not only the fighting capability of the German Wehrmacht but also
the risk of being thrown back into the sea from the beaches, or stagnating into a
First World War slugfest of horrific casualties for no territorial gain. However, led by
George Marshall, Roosevelt's most trusted military advisor, the American contingent
of commanders was confident in the belief that only by engaging the Germans in
northern France and driving into the German heartland would Nazi Germany be
defeated. Marshall not only believed in the policy but was confident that it would
succeed under the combined weight of Allied strength and force of commitment.
Therefore, due to the ever-growing build-up of American manpower and arms, the

impatient emphasis on invading France was gradually gaining traction. Dwarfing the British contribution, this American dominance in men, material and resources would leverage the British into a policy-making back seat, both strategically and tactically. The burgeoning thrust of American energy to invade France shifted into high gear and became not just American policy, but the overall Allied policy – whether Churchill and the British approved or not. For Roosevelt and Marshall, the invasion of France and assault on Hitler's vaunted Fortress Europe was to be the only policy that mattered. The appointment of Eisenhower as the commander of the cross-Channel assault underscored the depth of American commitment and investment, and the sooner it commenced, the quicker the war would be brought to an end.

For the post of supreme commander, Churchill had favoured his own top military advisor, the Chief of the Imperial General Staff (CIGS), General Sir Alan Brooke. Roosevelt assuredly felt that George Marshall deserved and could handle such a responsibility. But neither Brooke nor Marshall would be chosen. For Brooke it was an openly crushing decision, affecting his personality and career trajectory. But as Churchill pointed out, and Brooke reluctantly agreed, it was to be an 'American show'. Eisenhower had never been predicted as a choice for supreme commander, but his selection instead of Marshall had practical reasoning behind it. Roosevelt required someone in Washington who could manage the entire war effort, and in Marshall FDR possessed such a uniquely qualified individual. Marshall, of whom FDR said, 'I could not sleep at ease if [he] were out of Washington', was the man who FDR needed in Washington at all times.[1] Ever the loyal soldier and advisor, Marshall concurred and Eisenhower became supreme commander of the D-Day invasion.

In late 1943, Roosevelt and Churchill agreed that spring 1944 would be the date set for the invasion. In December 1943, FDR also announced that with Marshall's firm recommendation, it would be Eisenhower in the supreme command position. This announcement partially pacified the anxious Stalin, who had again questioned the resolve of Britain and the US for want of a definite date and a commanding officer for the invasion. This then settled the questions of when it would occur and who would be in charge.

Prior to the Second World War, Eisenhower had never led troops in combat. During the Second World War, Marshall recognised Eisenhower's talents and potential, successively advancing him as chief of operations, then commander of European Theatre Operations, and eventually commander of Operation Torch – the invasion of North Africa. This was followed quickly by the elevation to supreme commander for the invasion of Sicily and then Italy, and finally chief of Western Allied Operations in Europe. Eisenhower's meteoric rise and string of successes then led to his appointment by Marshall and approval by FDR as the supreme commander for the Overlord invasion.

Eisenhower, though lacking combat experience, was brilliant at organisation and administration. Combining this with his naturally genial personality, he became particularly adept at getting co-commanders to work together. This was critically important when dealing with the British and French commanders who would be serving with him. Diplomacy, compromise and leadership would be his strongest attributes and the most critically important features of his success. Carrying out such a huge operation as Overlord would take superior diplomatic, organisational and administrative skills that involved meshing a wide range of divergent personalities, egos and talents. In this, Eisenhower was unfailing. He is sometimes criticised for lacking bold tactical awareness and imagination, but his selection of high-quality operational field commanders easily outweighs that rebuke. Eisenhower was ruthless in the dismissal of officers who could not, or would not, perform to his full expectations. Correctly choosing capable subordinates who functioned as a battle-winning team was of paramount importance. To this strength Eisenhower added patience, skill and at times even genius. Many critics have claimed that Eisenhower lacked depth in tactical and strategic initiative, but his ability to successfully plan and execute the greatest amphibious invasion in history, while merging a multinational military operation, took incredible talent, initiative and leadership.

Adroitly filling his staff with a mix of British and American officers, Eisenhower went beyond mere window dressing. He sought and followed the advice of his commanders, even those who were less than congenial in their personalities, such as the vain and arrogant British General Sir Bernard Montgomery. Difficult to get along with, even among his fellow British commanders, Montgomery was appreciated by Eisenhower for his methodical preparation and tactical battlefield sense. Eisenhower named Montgomery as the overall ground commander for the invasion and readily agreed with Montgomery that the original invasion plan was too narrow and would need to be widened to include two more beaches and two more divisions. Such was the trust that Eisenhower placed in his staff.

With the full confidence of Roosevelt's appointment, coupled with Marshall's enthusiastic recommendation, Eisenhower now began selecting those who would assist him in the endless logistical and tactical details for the upcoming invasion. It would be necessary to meld both American and British officers into these vital positions; it would also be important to find room for the leaders of the Free French Army, since it was France that was going to be invaded and trampled upon by the Allied army. Liberation was important, but so too was French participation in the actual event, and this would require involving their self-proclaimed leader, the onerous and vainglorious General Charles de Gaulle.

Eisenhower quickly and liberally assembled a mix of British and American officers in his upper echelon invasion team – pleasing and satisfying both Roosevelt and Churchill. Developing a positive relationship with Britain's Prime Minister would be essential. Although they frequently disagreed on both policy and method, they retained a mutual trust and respect that included an amiable fondness for each other. In his instructions to Eisenhower, Marshall was explicit: Eisenhower could request any officers he required, and his appointments would be fully backed up; however, Ike was not to hesitate in the removal of any officer he felt inadequate to the task at hand or who failed to meet his satisfaction. Eisenhower would receive full support in his requests for subordinates, manpower and resources.

For his Deputy Supreme Commander, Eisenhower chose British Air Chief Marshal Sir Arthur Tedder. Air power would be vital in all stages of the invasion, and it was essential to have an airman backing up requests on tactics and allotted resources. Disputes over the use and command of air power for the invasion would be bitter and constant, but in the end, Eisenhower and the invasion requirements would get the nod.

Eisenhower chose as Chief of Staff his own personal friend and confidant, Major General Walter Bedell ('Beetle') Smith. Smith was thorough, professional and efficient, respected by all for his excellence. The Assistant Chief of Staff would be the British General Sir Frederick Morgan, who had formerly headed up the invasion planning committee before the appointment of Eisenhower.

For his Army Group Commander on the ground, Eisenhower chose the pompous and egotistical British General Sir Bernard Montgomery. Ike and Monty had clashed before, but it could not be denied that Monty was a dedicated and meticulous tactical planner. Even though Churchill was at times exasperated by him, Monty had won the Battle of El Alamein against the Germans in North Africa, and Churchill and the British were desperate for victories over the Germans. To Montgomery would go the task of planning the details of the beach landings and troop depositions – the bread and butter of the entire invasion plan. For all of his personality faults, most observers, Ike included, respected Montgomery's dedicated battlefield qualities.

Eisenhower chose British Air Chief Marshal Sir Trafford Leigh-Mallory to be in charge of the Allied invasion air forces and British Admiral Sir Bertram Ramsey to be in charge of the vital naval arm of the invasion forces. It had been Ramsey who had coordinated the rescue of the British Army from Dunkirk, France, in the spring of 1940 and he would now organise the Allies' naval armada to re-cross the English Channel and return to France.

Eisenhower's shrewd appointment of British officers for the top three command posts (ground, air and naval) did much to assuage Churchill and other British senior officers that Eisenhower was going to be fair and pragmatic in his selections for the combined operation. The individual army groups would retain their own national identities and officers, but the vast overall operation would be combined under one single upper command, the Chief of Staff, Supreme Allied Headquarters (COSSAC), now to be renamed Supreme Headquarters, Allied Expeditionary Force (SHAEF), of which Eisenhower assumed command.

Eisenhower and his team were also aware of the need for deception as to where they intended to land and used the hard-driving but controversial General George Patton to lead a phantom army, the designated 'American First Army'. This fake force would put on open and visible displays in southern England as part of the ongoing ruse to confuse the Germans as to the intended landing point in France. Considerable effort was engaged to convince Hitler and the German high command that the Allied invasion was to be directly across the Strait of Dover at the port of Calais – the nearest point from Britain. The Germans would never give up on the belief that the Allies would be landing at the Pas de Calais, and the Allies did everything in their power to encourage this belief. If the Germans were to hold back much of their defending force in the belief that Normandy was the deception, then the taking and holding of the Normandy beaches, although difficult, would be less so than it might have been. To this end, American General George Patton would command this 'ghost' army, and would openly display his presence near the fake encampment of his pretend army near the Strait of Dover. The Germans believed Patton to be the best of the American field generals, and therefore would erroneously conclude that Patton's army and presence were legitimate, reinforcing the deception.

GERMANY

The German leadership can be briefly summed up by their leader, Adolf Hitler. Hitler made policy, hired, fired and re-hired his commanders in a continuous circus of appointments. It was, of course, Hitler who had plunged Europe into war in 1939, and then foolishly jeopardised his successful conquest of western and central Europe with his ill-advised invasion of Soviet Russia in June 1941. Hitler continued to plague his generals through his maniacal decisions that went counter to almost all of his subordinate commanders' advice and recommendations. It was clear that war in the east against the Soviets was virtually doomed, and that if an Allied invasion of France was successful there would be no hope for victory, or even a negotiated peace, but only an inevitable defeat.

Hitler certainly understood the necessity of keeping the Allies out of Western Europe – but how to do this was the question. Most of his advisors strongly believed that the Allied attack would indeed come at the Pas de Calais, although Hitler himself was unsure and therefore demanded that his reinforcing forces wait for his word before engaging. This went completely contrary to the advice of Hitler's chosen commander for the defence of France against Allied invasion, Field Marshal Erwin Rommel. Rommel, the 'Desert Fox', was a veteran commander famous for his Blitzkrieg tactics early in the war against France and his dynamic leadership in North Africa against the British while leading his famous Afrika Korps. Rommel believed that the invasion would have to be defeated on the beaches. If the Allies achieved a foothold, there would be no denying them victory and the war would be lost. To this end, Rommel's plan to defend France, or Hitler's so-called Fortress Europe, would be to make the beaches as difficult as possible to land at, and to then immediately engage the assault as forcefully as possible in order to drive the Allies back into the sea. These defences would consist of mines, shore obstacles, concrete bunkers, barbed wire and multiple gun emplacements of all types. It would be manned by twenty divisions of various strength and experience, scattered the length of the Atlantic coast. The command of other German divisions would be retained by Hitler and other group commanders. This mammoth 200-mile project remained in the midst of preparation and construction as the Allied invasion arrived in June 1944.

The Germans under Rommel had already laid over 6.5 million mines and numerous steel-reinforced concrete bunkers. But the length of French coast was far too long, the time required too limited and – most important of all – the manpower and resources required to construct enough bunkers and obstacles for completion were sorely lacking. There was also the desperate need for experienced soldiers to man the beach outposts. Castoffs, foreign enlistees, forced labourers, recovering wounded and re-fitting regiments littered the defensive barracks. Worse still for Rommel and the Germans was the limited pool of first-rate soldiers available anywhere – for Germany the numbers were just no longer there.

Respecting his oncoming adversaries, Rommel commented, 'Our friends from the East [generals in Berlin and those fighting the Soviet armies on the Eastern front, who to Rommel were out of touch with reality] cannot imagine what they're in for here. It's not a matter of fanatical hordes to be driven forward in masses against our line, with no regard for casualties and little recourse to tactical craft...'[2] After assuming command of shore defences, Rommel was obsessed with the challenge of defending the entire length of the French coast from north of Calais along the North Sea to the southern end of the Bay of Biscay north of Spain, even though he realised his forces and resources were hopelessly inadequate to the task. Nonetheless, Rommel diligently pursued his belief in tank traps, steel beach obstacles and tens of thousands of buried landmines and obstacle-mounted mines. For Rommel, it was either defeat the Allies on the beach or be defeated.

German generals, Rommel included, frequently quarrelled with Hitler; Rommel also clashed with his immediate supervisor, Field Marshal Gerd von Rundstedt, on the positioning of the reinforcing units and how soon to engage a beach invasion. They all agreed that moving the reserves to engage a deception would be tantamount to a defeat. This issue was never conclusively resolved by the German high command. Of the two schools of thought, Rommel's was probably correct, although it required a 'Fortress' approach for every beach and stretch of French coast – an almost impossible task. The flexible plan of von Rundstedt and Heinz Guderian, another leading German general and frequent challenger to Hitler's tactics, involved holding back the major force of defending Panzer units until it became clear just where the actual invasion strength was centred. This certainly required fewer beach defences but, conversely, greater unit manpower numbers in order to attain a superior concentration of force when implemented. It also, of course, risked the critical element of time in order to identify where and to what degree the Allies were attacking, and then to rapidly implement attack thrusts at the points of invasion when they were correctly identified. Most importantly, it required sufficient strength in depth to defeat a rapidly reinforcing army of invaders. Another major fault in this strategy was the Allies' complete control of the air. Limited only by bad weather, at all times the Allies were assured of tactical and strategic air advantage with their bombers, fighters and fighter-bombers – the Allies owned the air. No German military units could move on the ground without being observed and risking immediate obliteration. Assuming the idea to hold back the reserve Panzer units was correct, there was no way to safely advance them to the point of attack. Any movement would expose their location and initiate a hurricane of withering fire from the air. The German air force, the

Luftwaffe, was now virtually non-existent and had little or nothing to offer in the form of resistance against the overwhelming Allied air superiority. With this in mind, Rommel's tactics were probably the most practical and correct form to adhere to.

This conflict of viewpoints was never settled and the confusion on the part of the Germans was greater than the Allied confusion upon landing – and certainly worked to the Allies' benefit. By failing to fully commit to either strategy, the Germans virtually ensured failure in their primary goal: to defend Europe from a successful Allied invasion. For the Allies, as slender and as risky as they viewed their overall chances of success, their imagination in preparation before the invasion, and their determination when entering the fighting on the beaches, never wavered.

UTAH BEACH COMMAND

The British command of the eastern beaches, labelled Gold, Sword and Juno, would have a separate set of naval, infantry and airborne commanders while remaining under the unified command of Eisenhower and his SHAEF staff. Likewise, the American sector or western beaches, consisting of Omaha Beach, Utah Beach and Pont du Hoc, was also under overall SHAEF command, although the immediate direct command was given to Lieutenant General Omar Bradley. Bradley had been Eisenhower's trusted battlefield commander during the Mediterranean campaigns and his 'western beaches group' was designated First US Army. Bradley's First US Army was then

German Field Marshal Erwin Rommel, 'The Desert Fox', shown here in North Africa where he had demonstrated his talent for mobile armoured warfare. Rommel had been personally selected by Hitler to strengthen Fortress Europa, Hitler's vaunted Atlantic Wall defending against the Allied invasion of Western Europe. In the six months leading up to D-Day he notably increased the strength of the defences, especially through the liberal use of mines and obstacles. (LOC)

divided under two component commanders: Major General J. Lawton Collins would head the Utah infantry and airborne landings, conducted by his VII Corps, and Major General Leonard T. Gerow's V Corps would land at nearby Omaha Beach. The US naval commander assigned to bombard the western beaches and land the American forces was Admiral Alan Kirk. Kirk's western task force was again divided into two forces: the Omaha sector headed by Admiral John Hall and the Utah sector headed by Admiral Don Moon.

With these naval task forces in place, the crossing of the English Channel and landing the Allied forces, code-named Operation Neptune, was about to begin. This would inaugurate the long-planned D-Day invasion. Operation Overlord was ready to commence.

Operation Overlord's infantry high command. In the center is the overall commander of ground forces, Bernard Montgomery, flanked by Omar Bradley (left), commander of US ground forces, and Thomas Dempsey, commander of British ground forces. Bradley had been General Eisenhower's lead commander in the North Africa campaign and would remain in command of US ground forces for Operation Overlord. Throughout D-Day morning, the critically desperate situation on Omaha Beach led Bradley to consider withdrawing. (US Army)

Eisenhower and his chief deputies for Operation Overlord. Back row, left to right: Omar Bradley, Bertram Ramsey, Trafford Leigh-Mallory, Walter 'Beetle' Smith. Front row, left to right: Arthur Tedder, Dwight Eisenhower and Bernard Montgomery. Eisenhower made it a point to liberally incorporate British officers into his command team. Tedder, a British air chief marshal, became Eisenhower's choice as deputy commander of Operation Overlord. Eisenhower understood the importance of air superiority for the D-Day effort, and Tedder became essential to Ike's command team. (US Navy)

General Dwight D. Eisenhower. Eisenhower had never commanded large forces until his rapid rise during the Second World War. For Eisenhower it was imperative that his commanders exude only confidence and optimism in the Overlord project. His administrative and diplomatic talents were outstanding, especially in the role of supreme commander for Operation Overlord. He would later be twice elected as US President on the strength of his wartime successes. (US Army)

Above left: General Joseph ('Lightning Joe') Collins, commander of American ground forces on Utah Beach for D-Day. Collins was a veteran commander of several amphibious invasions of Pacific islands. (US Army)

Above right: General Walter 'Beetle' Smith, Eisenhower's chief of staff for Operation Overlord. Smith was highly regarded and respected by both the American and British high commands. (US Army)

Admiral Sir Bertram Ramsey, Eisenhower's supreme naval commander for Operation Neptune, the vital crossing of the English Channel and landings for Operation Overlord. Ramsey had already won great fame and plaudits for his achievement in rescuing the defeated British Army from Dunkirk in 1940. (NARA)

Britain's military high command: Generals Alan Brooke (left) and Bernard Montgomery (right) and British Prime Minister Winston Churchill (centre). Churchill and Brooke remained dubious and hesitant about the Overlord mission and its risks. Brooke and Churchill were also reluctant to concede that the war was becoming a larger and increasingly American operation due to the mountains of equipment and supplies being provided, and the rapidly increasing size of the US Army. Brooke thought himself a complete realist towards strategy in general and Overlord in particular. He was forever reining Churchill in from his wilder schemes. Brooke, like Marshall, desired to be the supreme commander of Operation Overlord and was bitterly disappointed to be denied this position. He remained Churchill's chief military advisor through most of the Second World War. (US Army)

Admiral Alan Kirk was in charge of the US naval operations for the western sector of Operation Overlord – the naval component being Operation Neptune and the crossing of the English Channel to land US forces on Omaha and Utah Beaches. (US Navy)

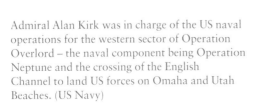

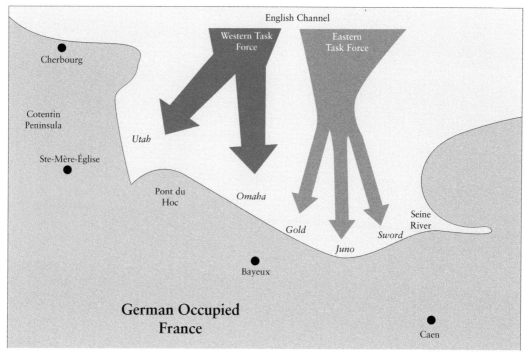

Operation Neptune ferried the Allied assault teams across the imposing English Channel, supported the five beaches with heavy bombardment and delivered the invasion forces into France.

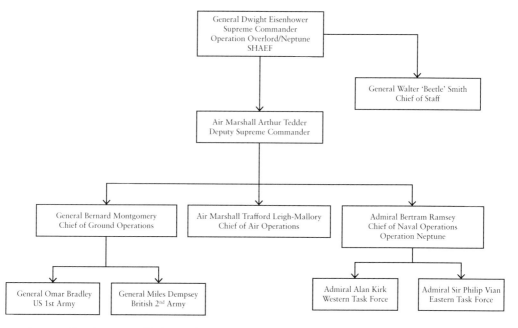

Supreme Headquarters Allied Expeditionary Force (SHAEF) command structure.

Chapter 4

German Defences

Once defeated, the enemy will never try to invade again … an invasion failure would deliver a crushing blow to British and American morale.

Adolf Hitler

During the Napoleonic wars a century and a half before the Second World War, Napoleon Bonaparte had sadly realised that the English Channel would prevent his French Grande Armée from attempting to invade and conquer England. Early in the Second World War, when Great Britain was at its most vulnerable and Germany at its strongest, the English Channel had kept the Germans from invading and possibly conquering the island nation. Now in 1944, German Field Marshal Erwin Rommel believed the situation was reversed. The key to victory in the defence of Hitler's Atlantic Wall would be the necessity for the Allies to cross the storm-tossed Channel and establish a position on the French coast. As a result of this, Field Marshal Rommel recognised the English Channel as his first and best line of defence. He therefore concentrated his maximum defensive preparation toward keeping the Allies in the water and off the beaches. When the Allies hit the beaches, the single aim of the Germans would be to drive them back into the sea and prevent them from developing a beachhead of opportunity. A successful beach landing would allow the Allies to reinforce in depth and mass. For Rommel, if the Allies were to secure a beachhead position, then the battle, and the war, would be lost. It would only be a matter of time until the stronger and logistically superior Allied forces drove the Germans back into Germany – and to inevitable defeat and surrender.

Maintaining control of the beaches and keeping the assaulting army at sea would be the primary task and the only guarantee of preventing defeat. Rommel had been quoted as emphasising the importance of the beach defence and expressing the opinion: 'The first twenty-four hours of the invasion will be decisive … the fate of Germany depends on the outcome. For the Allies as well as Germany, it will be the longest day.'[3]

Rommel had been selected to organise Hitler's Atlantic Wall against an Allied invasion in the late autumn of 1943. He began by examining where the invasion might fall, how to defend those positions and constructing as rapidly as possible the means to blunt such an attack. To this end, Rommel identified large stores of French explosives that could be quickly converted to landmines. The majority of these mines were designed to be detonated under the weight of a man or vehicle, others by a trip wire. German Teller mines were saucer-shaped discs, roughly a foot in diameter, designed to explode under the weight of a tank or heavy vehicle. Many of these devilish devices had anti-tamper mechanisms, causing them to explode if moved or lifted. The laying of several million mines was accompanied by the installation of tens of thousands of obstacles, both steel and wood, to prevent landing craft from getting through the surf and onto the beaches. The steel obstacles, meant to prevent landing craft from nearing the inner beach area, lay over 100 yards beyond the low tide point. Wooden poles were then planted at protruding angles and sunk closer to the seawall to present the same problem to any landing craft able to negotiate closer to the shore. These obstacles were draped with anti-personnel mines and anti-vehicle mines (to defend against both tanks and landing craft) and were planted by the millions along the French coast. Not designed for salt water, many of these mines would deteriorate and be unable to detonate due to their prolonged exposure to the conditions of the Channel surf.

The Channel approaches to the beaches and the waters of the English Channel more generally were also littered with anti-ship mines of all types: contact mines that required a ship or boat to come into contact with them – especially useful in shallow waters and often near a beach; magnetic mines that detonated on sensing the metal hull of a nearby ship; concussion/pressure mines that sensed the movement of an object such as a nearby passing ship; and acoustic mines that detonated in response to a ship's propeller noise. These mines were usually floating or anchored at different depths to discourage detection.

Rommel was in the process of increasing this massive mine-laying campaign when D-Day actually arrived. He had already tripled the number of mines on the beach coasts and was hurriedly planting and laying hundreds of thousands more. His mine-laying was of course not just limited to Normandy but was spread across every potential invasion beach. Immediately upon Rommel's taking command, the rate of mines being laid every month went from 40,000 when he arrived to over a million. By mid-May, over 4 million mines had been laid. Even so, by June of 1944, Rommel realised that there were not nearly enough mines in place to fulfil his defensive requirements.

Rommel also sought a dramatic increase in the planting of wooden, steel and concrete obstacles (hedgehogs) to impede landing craft and to which were attached larger mines. By mid-May, over half a million new obstacles of various sizes and shapes had been installed. Behind these formidable beach obstacles were ground troops who would actually be called upon to do the fighting. Rommel insisted on greater numbers to man the beach garrisons and more reinforcing armoured units to back them up. To boost morale, Rommel made frequent inspection visits to encourage confidence among his Atlantic Wall defenders. Most of these units were a hodgepodge of over-aged or under-aged recruits: work crews constructing the beach defences; armoured units refitting from the Eastern front; and the ground crews no longer needed by the practically defunct German air forces. There were also foreign volunteer units from prisoner of war camps on the Russian front. However, as motley as they may have appeared on paper, many of these units would put up stiff resistance on D-Day. In particular, Rommel counted heavily on the rapid deployment of the experienced Panzer units being held in reserve.

A realist, Rommel recognised the grim truth of other compelling facts and figures. He understood that he would have little to no air support, as by June 1944 the Allies outnumbered the Germans in aircraft by over 100 to 1. On D-Day, the Allies were able to place into the sky more than 9,500 airplanes of all makes and sizes, against a total German contingent of less than 900.[4] An incredible disparity of force! Rommel therefore concentrated on the fixed defences, which included concrete and steel-reinforced bunkers, pillboxes and heavy gun emplacements. Behind the seawall of the beach were bands of barbed and concertina wire. Near the beaches, ridges or bluffs, all local buildings such as civilian dwellings, beach houses and boat sheds were destroyed to reduce any and all cover for the assaulting soldiers. Those buildings that remained were converted into machine-gun nests and shelters for the defending artillery.

Rommel had also correctly envisioned that the Allies might attempt to land airborne soldiers either by parachute or glider, which in fact the Allies did. To meet this threat and hinder this form of attack, Rommel flooded pastures and open areas and planted barriers in farm fields and meadows. Like most of the German Atlantic Wall efforts, the installations were spread too thin and remained incomplete by June 1944. However, many Allied gliders were demolished on landing when they ran into Rommel's 'asparagus' trees sprouting out of otherwise open pastures. To hem in any would-be breakout by a successful landing, the Germans used local streams and rivers to flood the area behind Utah Beach into a marsh of shallow lakes, impeding the landing of airborne units and blocking a rapid breakout by assault forces.

Hitler's inevitable meddling in troop dispositions led to a compromised three-pronged separation of mobile Panzer units to defend over 500 miles of coastline. Hitler himself doubted the Pas de Calais would be the likely point of invasion and believed the Allies would choose an alternative location. He fully understood the importance of the invasion when he issued his Fuhrer Order Number 51, declaring:

> ... A greater danger now appears in the west; an Anglo-Saxon landing! ... Should the enemy succeed in breeching our defences on a wide front here, the immediate consequences would be unpredictable. Everything indicates that the enemy will launch an offensive...at the latest in the spring, perhaps even earlier ... I have therefore decided to reinforce its defences...[5]

Rommel was given command of three mobile Panzer divisions that he kept close to the coast; his counterpart, General Leo Geyr von Sweppenburg, was also given three mobile Panzer divisions to be placed in tactical reserve. Von Sweppenburg believed, correctly as it turned out, that the Allies could not be stopped on the beaches but only through a fierce and concentrated counter-attack. Rommel feared, also correctly, that the reinforcing units would not arrive in time to alter the situation. Rommel argued that any counterattacking units would be severely hampered, if not destroyed, by the superior Allied air power. Finally, Hitler himself retained four divisions in strategic reserve, to be summoned when it was conclusively identified where the invasion was taking place and when to apply the necessary counter stroke. It was not what Rommel desired, but it was what he was forced to accept.

Rommel was clearly going to roll the dice in defeating the Allies on the beach, but the enduring problem for the German defenders was which beach in France, and when. Due to Hitler's overly zealous desire for conquest around the world, the Third Reich was now undermanned and on the defensive. For Rommel and the Germans, the effort to defend Fortress Europe was now a problem of too little time and too few resources for far too much beach.

The dreaded and potent German 88 mm all-purpose anti-aircraft flak gun. This notorious weapon proved to be a devastating anti-tank gun and was much respected by the Allies. (RJP)

Thousands of these steel 'hedgehog' obstacles were placed along French beaches, both above and below the tideline, to impede landing craft. (RJP)

The Germans constructed hundreds of these concrete bunker gun emplacements along the French coast. (NARA)

Many German guns were housed in armoured turrets protected within concrete bunkers. These bunkers housed barracks and troop facilities. (NARA)

German soldiers moving to the front to meet the Allies' D-Day invasion. German defenders in France consisted of a very mixed lot: the very young and very old recruits, recovering wounded, volunteer POWs from the Eastern Front and some crack Panzer units on refits. (NARA)

A German Jagdpanzer IV armoured tank destroyer equipped with a 7.5 cm main gun. (RJP)

Thousands of these tetrahedral concrete beach obstacles peppered the French coastline to impede landing craft. Many were topped with mines. (RJP)

Thousands of these timber pole obstacles, many equipped with mines, littered the French beaches and accommodated both low and high sea levels. (NARA)

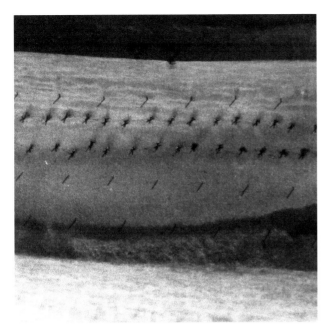

Above left: An aerial view of the German beach obstacles along the French coast. (NARA)

Above right: German Teller mines mounted on beach obstacles. (NARA)

German soldiers erecting timber pole beach obstacles along the French coast. (NARA)

Chapter 5

Overlord Deception

In wartime the truth is so precious that she should be attended by a bodyguard of lies.

British Prime Minister Winston Churchill

Operation Bodyguard, the multiple programmes designated to conceal the true location and dates of the upcoming beach landings, was absolutely vital to the success of Operation Overlord. In the Allies' favour was the fact that most German military leaders were betting on the Pas de Calais as the probable invasion site. It certainly would have been a logical choice. The French port of Calais lay directly across the Strait of Dover, less than 25 miles (35 kilometres) from Britain. Its location would allow for masses of soldiers to be transported and protected by air and water. It would also permit the resupply of the enormous amount of provisions an invading army would require. None of these advantages were lost on the Germans. Because of this incorrect deduction on their part, the Pas de Calais was given a much stronger German defence than other potential sites.

In order to continue the deception that Calais would be the point of invasion, the Allies went to great lengths to persuade the Germans that this indeed was their plan. For example, during weeks of pre-invasion bombing, Allied forces purposely focused more than necessary on the Pas de Calais and its surrounding area. The Germans, not knowing it was meant as a distraction, deduced that the air strikes were meant to soften up their defences before an imminent attack there. In an attempt to further confuse the enemy concerning their plans, additional targets were chosen for bombing missions. Many were selected in France, while others were as far north as Scandinavia.

Because it was of the utmost importance to keep the true D-Day plans an extremely well- guarded secret, the Allies put significant energy into additional methods of deception that involved even more trickery. Much of this involved feeding false information to the Nazis, a feat that was sometimes accomplished in blatant ways like transmitting radio messages that were unashamed lies. Some fabricated 'secret information' was fed back to Germany through its own spy network. German spies who were identified early in the war and coerced to act as double agents sent back false narratives to their headquarters. One of the more macabre ploys was to actually use a dead body disguised as a fallen soldier, spy, or diplomat carrying hints of information related to D-Day. After placing fake documents on the body, it would be strategically placed where the enemy was sure to find it. The goal was to confuse the Germans and distort the truth in whatever way possible.

Of all the clandestine efforts that could tip the war in the Allies' favour, one of the most significant and highly guarded secrets was the work being done by Alan Turing, one of the early fathers of computer science, and the other code-breakers at Bletchley Park. The Nazis had taken the art of encryption to a new level, using their Enigma cypher machine to secure their coded messages. The Allies were able to intercept these secret messages, but decoding them had proven to be a discouragingly difficult task. Harnessing some of the best minds in the field, the British government vigorously supported the Herculean task of finding a way to decipher the ever-changing puzzle. The code was eventually broken, although it was a time-consuming effort. Tragically, the Allies could not act on all of the uncovered information for fear of tipping their hand. If the Germans suspected their Enigma cipher had been cracked, they would surely turn to another method of encryption, wiping out months and months of work and landing the British code-breakers back at square one. The knowledge of this breakthrough was limited to a select few, and only at the highest leadership levels of Britain and America. The information garnered was referred to as Ultra by the British and Magic by the US; even top leaders who received some of this information never learned of its true source. As for the Germans, they remained unaware throughout the remainder of the war that the Allies were able to translate these heretofore secret messages. By 1941, German naval signals were being deciphered and used to direct some Allied ships away from areas that were most heavily threatened by German U-boats. The ability to interpret signals to and between the U-boats would have a hugely positive impact on vital transatlantic shipping and the upcoming D-Day invasion.

As D-Day drew near, the risk of a breach in the secrecy of the Overlord plan became heightened. Since more than 150,000 soldiers would be involved and training missions were already taking place, the need to keep even these troops unaware of the invasion details was clear. They were not informed of the day or the specific beaches where the assault would take place. In fact, in the months preceding the attack, bogus location names were used during military drills, keeping the number of individuals with knowledge of the accurate details to a bare minimum. Although encouraged by the lack of any evidence that the plans had been divulged, Allied intelligence officers continually sought out any sign that spies or leaks had somehow revealed the true location of the planned invasion to the Germans. The effort could not have been greater and the stakes could not have been higher.

Another major ruse by Allied Command was put into play. Code-named Operation Fortitude, a cinematic-style deception was implemented in southern England, where troops were gathering at a faux base, complete with mock-up replicas of army barracks, tanks, planes and all manner of military equipment. Adding to the authenticity, American General George Patton himself was brought in to lead the drills, be seen and provide colourful appearances and speeches to the local community and press. German commanders, well aware of Patton's résumé and skills, had incorrectly anticipated that he would lead the invasion into France. His presence across the Strait of Dover, along with all of the fake equipment, could be observed by German forces ensconced in the Pas de Calais, leading the Nazis to falsely conclude beyond any reasonable doubt that the attack would indeed take place at Calais, and it would be led by General Patton. Before long, they would be proven wrong on both counts.

By June 1944, virtually all German military leaders were convinced that a major Allied invasion would be attempted at the Pas de Calais. This was true all the way up the chain of command, although Hitler maintained a deep suspicion of Calais and sensed that the Allies might strike elsewhere. Because all signs had pointed that way for so long, in German minds it became a fact rather than merely a prediction, and German defences echoed this belief. Even as the D-Day invasion unfolded, the Nazis still suspected the attack at Normandy might actually be a diversion preceding the 'true' assault at Calais. This delay in response would prove disastrous for the Germans. A successful counterattack depends on a quick, powerful retaliation. With too many troops assembled in the area around Calais, and with the German command wavering on whether to immediately send troops for a counteroffensive, the Nazis lost their opportunity. Aided by the brilliant deciphering of German intercepts and the devious deceptions carried out for months by Allied leaders, the impact of Operation Bodyguard on the success of the Operation Overlord plan cannot be either ignored or underestimated.

German Field Marshals von Rundstedt (left) and Rommel were both convinced the Allied invasion would take place somewhere near the French port of Calais. The phantom army ruse helped maintain this deception. (Bundesarchiv)

At the Bletchley Park decoding centre, prototype computer-like machines known as bombes would churn through the coded Enigma intercepts to ferret out German messages. (RJP)

Bletchley Park, the decoding and deciphering centre located in England, was instrumental in the breaking of the German Enigma messages. (RJP)

A German Enigma code machine. Throughout all of the Second World War the Germans believed their Enigma device to be impenetrable. This secret of the 'secrets' was also carefully guarded and maintained by the Allies. (RJP)

A fake balloon tank being easily lifted and moved. To confuse the Germans, phoney prop tanks, barracks and airplanes were all part of the deception to convince the Germans that General George Patton's fictitious army, known as FUSAG, was real and preparing to assault Calais. Patton would later command the real-life US Third Army in the drive through Europe. (LOC)

Chapter 6

Overlord Equipment

Here we are facing an enemy who applies all his native intelligence to the use of his main technical resources, who spares no expenditure of material and whose every operation goes its course as though it had been the subject of repeated rehearsal!
German Field Marshal Erwin Rommel commenting
on the technological methods and wealth of Britain and the US

The Germans could not be engaged and defeated in Europe until the invasion forces were ferried safely and securely to the French coast. A few of these smaller landing vessels, all with odd acronyms and nicknames, became the primary method of delivering an army of soldiers from naval transports to the shore. To meet this requirement, a variety of landing craft were designed, built and produced in extraordinary numbers. However, the need for ever more landing craft of all sizes remained a never-ending concern to the Overlord planners.

Large transports would carry the 150,000 Allied soldiers from their ports of embarkation and they would then be ferried on smaller boats to the shore. It was a perilous operation in the best of conditions, let alone under enemy gunfire. The English Channel is often beset by storms and treacherous currents; crossing it at any time can induce seasickness even in large, seaworthy ships. Depending upon their point of embarkation, the amphibious armada of large transports would cross between 50 and 100 miles of mine-infested English Channel to reach Normandy. Anchoring 10 to 15 miles from the Normandy coast, the troops would offload onto smaller landing craft of various sizes and types and ride through the storm-tossed surf. If not already sick from crossing the Channel, most would now become seasick as they awaited their fate of landing on the five D-Day beaches. Along with the smaller troop-carrying landing craft would also come larger landing craft carrying a wide array of armoured vehicles, equipment, weapons and ammunition. Some armoured military vehicles were designed to plough through the surf under their own power and navigation – many would fail to manage the journey and end up swamped, drowning their crew before firing a shot or even being shot at. Such were the hazards and challenges of amphibious operations.

First and foremost of the landing craft was the Higgins boat, the most widely built and used landing craft of any type. It was attached to the large transports and then loaded with soldiers for the ride to the beach. Besides personnel, these boats could also carry equipment, smaller vehicles or heavy weapons, or a combination. They were adaptable and ubiquitous. Usually labelled LCVP (Landing Craft, Vehicles and Personnel), they were designed by Andrew Higgins. The versatile Higgins boat was an inexpensive, self-propelled craft with a bow ramp for rapid unloading that dropped forward to release its cargo of men and equipment. The American version was made of wood, the British version of steel, and both models were used during D-Day. The US Navy had more than 1,000 LCVPs available for D-Day and almost 100 were sunk, over half of the losses coming on Omaha Beach alone. But at Utah Beach they survived in greater number.

Andrew Higgins had worked in the lumber business and developed a method of forming wood into waterproof surfaces that could then be crafted into powerful lightweight landing boats for the war effort. In 1940, his boat-building company was headquartered in New Orleans, Louisiana, and had already begun operation in anticipation of the need for such craft in the Second World War. His company eventually began assembling 700 landing boats per month to meet the enormous demand for amphibious landing craft. During the war, Higgins' company delivered over 20,000 landing craft. They were of three main types: the initial model, or LCP (Landing Craft Personnel), could carry thirty-six soldiers; the larger LCVP could carry thirty-six soldiers, 5 tons of cargo or a small vehicle; and a larger model still, the LCM (Landing Craft Mechanised), could handle 120 men, a medium tank or up to 30 tons of assorted equipment. His company also provided the wooden hulls for the navy's fast and versatile PT boats. Without these landing craft, the major amphibious landings against the Japanese-held Pacific islands, the Mediterranean landings and of course D-Day would have been problematic, if not impossible.

Once a beach was reasonably secured, it would be essential to have as many troops and armoured vehicles delivered as quickly as possible in order to develop the position in depth and penetrate inland. This endeavour required larger vessels for the offloading of vehicles and personnel onto a shore that was an active war zone. Perhaps the most important of this type was the Landing Ship Tank. The LST was a huge, flat-bottomed vessel with enormous twin doors in its bow and was purposely designed to carry several large vehicles, such as tanks and trucks, hence the name. LSTs were longer than a football field at over 300 ft in length, and although slow-moving at barely 10 knots, they could literally drive right up and onto a beach to disgorge heavy armour and vehicles directly onto the shore. These shallow-draft, double-floored behemoths could operate without proper ports by beaching their bows and opening their huge frontal doors to drop a ramp and begin unloading nearly three dozen trucks, or nearly two dozen medium tanks. Used all over the Pacific and Atlantic theatres of war, over 250 LSTs were employed at Normandy, delivering everything from troops, tanks and jeeps to heavy equipment. On withdrawal, they could then be used to carry wounded soldiers back across the English Channel. Their size, lack of speed and valuable cargo made them a vulnerable and plum target, particularly for warplanes, and several LSTs were sunk or damaged during the Overlord campaign.

Until an LST could safely unload a couple of dozen tanks at one time, the assaulting troops needed to rely on amphibious vehicles. The amphibious tanks and vehicles were of several designs, but all sought to accomplish the same thing: get high-powered armour and mobile weapons onto the beaches as soon as possible. It was a dangerous and difficult challenge and, unfortunately for many of the D-Day crews, a fatal one. The difficulty in getting tanks ashore early and in quantity also resulted in complications for the freshly landed soldiers, who were in desperate need of armoured support as they confronted the German defenders. This became a particular dilemma on Omaha Beach.

Allied commanders counted on a certain number of armoured vehicles, such as tanks and tank destroyers, to survive the distance between the transport vessels and the shore. On four of the five beaches, a sufficient number achieved this goal – on Utah they did, but on Omaha they did not. This was a hazardous journey for the heavy vehicles, as they were not designed to be amphibious. Numerous ideas were tested in order to deliver this extremely important function of providing immediate armoured support and protection for the ground troops wading ashore and crawling up the beach. This capability would be crucial to the success of engaging the dug-in German defenders.

Many schemes and ideas were literally floated for trial and experiment, including a skirt-like floatation device to keep out the surf while auxiliary propellers, powered by the tank's specially adapted 'Duplex-Drive' motor system, propelled the tank through the water. These tanks were then labelled as 'DD' for 'Duplex-Drive'. This DD amphibious version of the Sherman medium tank was developed to motor an armoured tank to the beach without being ferried by a landing craft. This would be particularly useful if these armoured vehicles could go in with the first group of assault units and provide both protection and firepower right from the earliest and most critical moments of the assaults.

Another form of independently arriving armoured vehicle was the 'wading tank' version of the Sherman tank. This formatted tank needed to be dropped off in shallow water, could fire its cannon from this position, and would then track its way onto the beach proper. It had been used by the army in both the Sicily and Salerno invasions and was the preferred amphibious armoured vehicle of numerous American commanding officers at Normandy. At Utah Beach, twenty-eight out of the initial thirty-two amphibious tanks successfully reached the beach.

Another variety was dubbed Hobart's Funnies, the term used for an assortment of armoured vehicles devised to survive the journey through the surf and onto the Normandy beaches in order to clear and improve beach passage conditions. Major General Percy Hobart was a British tank officer in charge of organising and training British tank divisions, but he was called upon to use his imagination and expertise with tanks to produce a means to deliver armoured vehicles safely through the surf off the coast of Normandy. Numerous ideas and methods were developed and experiments conducted, with the result being a variety of flotation devices and gadget vehicles. These 'Funnies' were designed for specific invasion tasks, and were built onto otherwise traditional armoured frames. Examples that were successful include American Sherman 'crab' tanks equipped with a revolving drum of flailing front end chains that whipped the ground, removing and discharging buried landmines or fence-mounted mines and barbed wire, thus clearing a path for following troops and vehicles; British Churchill tanks equipped with diabolical long-range flamethrowers; and utility tanks carrying coiled steel fencing for the laying of bridge work over culverts and ditches, or to lay stiffer roadway on the beaches themselves. All of these proved practical and useful.

One of the criticisms of the American command team, and General Bradley in particular, was their reluctance to accept advice on amphibious landing from either the British commanders or American officers from the Pacific theatre, all of whom had prior experience with amphibious vehicles and operations against sandy beaches defended by fanatically dedicated and well-equipped defenders. Bradley and his cohorts felt that the beaches of France were physically different and that the operational scale was much larger. The response to the British 'Funnies' was the implied belief that these were gadgets that did not merit further discussion or development. American Pacific commanders also recommended the use of armoured amphibious motorised vehicles (AMTRACs) to carry men and equipment ashore. AMTRACs were more seaworthy in rough water and able to operate both in water and on sandy beaches, besides having the obvious advantage of being armoured. Chief of Staff General George Marshall sent several veteran American Pacific commanders, both army and marine, to assist the Normandy invasion, but their expertise and experience was basically dismissed by the army preparing in Europe.

The British tested many odd and creative ideas for landing craft and were willing to experiment to a greater degree than the Americans. This reluctance faded when, later in the campaign, the US Army encountered the difficult Bocage hedgerows within the interior of the Normandy countryside. American GIs took it upon themselves to equip their Sherman tanks with former German steel beach obstacles and thus jerry-rig bocage penetrating fork-like prongs extending from the fronts of their tanks. It was an effective and efficient innovation. Unfortunately, the soldiers landing on Omaha were unable to adapt their vehicles to the immediate circumstances and were doomed to suffer the tragic consequences of shortcomings in their beach landing equipment.

SUPPLY

Obviously the need for port facilities was vital. Feeding, arming, maintaining and reinforcing what would soon be a 500,000-man army would take fantastic amounts of supplies. Cargo crossing the English Channel in transports would be stymied unless the ships had immediate access to a pier, dock or harbour in which to unload. LSTs could only carry so much. What the Allied effort demanded was a deep-water port that could handle ocean-going freighters to supply their titanic war effort. Since any European port seized would undoubtedly be destroyed by surrendering Germans, an alternative was sought and devised. In order to sustain the initial 150,000 assault troops securing their Normandy beachhead, and the thousands of reinforcements who were rapidly arriving to consolidate the position, plus the anticipated needs for the expected breakout into the interior of France, a port of some kind would be demanded. It would be two weeks before the port of Cherbourg was captured and another two months for its destroyed facilities to be repaired. The temporary answer would be the use of Mulberries.

Mulberries were mammoth portable floating docks that were ferried across the English Channel to be linked together near shore in order to provide a ready-made deep-water docking platform for transport ships unloading troops, vehicles and supplies. Backed by the staunch support of British Prime Minister Winston Churchill, the 600-ton floating prefabricated concrete shells were to be the main means of unloading larger ships until a full-scale port could be captured and repaired for fulltime operation. Two Mulberry harbours were inserted, one at Arromanches off the British Gold Beach, and an American one off Omaha beach. No Mulberries were destined for Utah Beach, relying instead on the Omaha Mulberry and the quick capture of the French port of Cherbourg. Both the American Mulberry and the captured port of Cherbourg, however, would remain unreliable in the near term.

The Mulberries were an extraordinary invention and accomplishment in both an engineering and practical sense. Unfortunately, the American Mulberry at Omaha Beach was destroyed by a ferocious Atlantic storm shortly after its installation. 200 LSTs provided temporary landing capacity and the hopelessly damaged American Mulberry was never repaired. The British Mulberry survived the storm and became an essential and, for a while, virtually the only docking facility on the Normandy coast. This remained true until late July 1944, when the port of Cherbourg was sufficiently repaired to be available for limited operation. Assisting the Mulberry harbour was a line of obsolete vessels purposely sunk around it to provide a protective breakwater. Completing the portable port was an ingeniously designed floating roadway, which would rise and fall with the tide and extended to connect the Mulberry unit with the beach. The Mulberry engineering teams began work almost immediately on D-Day+2 and soon formed a harbour 2 miles long and 1 mile wide, with enough docking space to handle up to seven supply ships at one time. Half a million troops, hundreds of tons of equipment and supplies, and 80,000 vehicles were offloaded via the Mulberry harbour.[6] Remnants of the derelict Mulberry units and the adjoining breakwater hulks can still be seen offshore at Arromanches to this day.

SPECIALITY AIR

In order to tow gliders and drop paratroopers behind Utah and Sword Beaches, the workhorse of the Allied air transport units was called upon in great number. The plane to carry out this mission was the twin-engine Douglas C-47 Dakota/Skytrain. Introduced in 1935, the revolutionary C-47 (Douglas DC-3) had been the first truly conventional commercial passenger aircraft before the war, and was still in service around the world nearly half a century later. Although not fast, it was stable in flight, ruggedly built, dependable and capable of a multitude of Second World War transport missions, including various speciality roles such as the Normandy paratrooper operations.

The C-47 would be employed to drop paratroopers and for towing a variety of gilders carrying troops, weapons and heavy equipment. The G-4 Waco, the main glider used by the American airborne divisions during the D-Day invasions, could hold thirteen soldiers, or a jeep and its crew, or a compact 75 mm howitzer and crew. It was built with a steel tube frame and featured a hinged front hatch to lift the entire front portion of the cockpit for ease of loading. The ability to bring in small vehicles, mortars and howitzers proved beneficial in the early stages of the invasion when resupply was of critical importance. Over 12,000 Waco gliders were manufactured during the war and more than 300 were employed behind Utah Beach for the initial D-Day invasion.

THE SPECIALITY WEAPONS

Dozens of speciality weapons were developed for the Allied amphibious invasions and one of the most common and effective was the Bangalore torpedo. Bangalore torpedoes were long tubes laden with explosives and used to remove obstacles and barbed wire. Their length could be extended by adding numerous pipe-like extensions and sliding the completed tube under or near the object to be blasted; a long fuse would then detonate the explosives. They were used frequently on the D-Day beaches by soldiers who were otherwise pinned down by gunfire.

Flamethrowers were used extensively and effectively to root out defenders hidden in bunkers, but the first assault troops to arrive carrying these lethal and highly flammable fluid-laden devices were extremely vulnerable to catastrophic results in attempting to struggle their way onto a tightly held beach or position. Tanks with long-range flame-throwing capability would have a devastating effect as the troops moved inland through the Bocage of interior rural France.

The Douglas C-47 (DC-3) Skytrain/ Dakota. Dependable and durable, the C-47 was a workhorse in all theatres of the Second World War, but at Utah Beach it was given the added responsibility of dropping thousands of paratroopers via parachute and landing by towed glider. (US Army)

The M-4 Sherman tank, produced in huge numbers by US factories throughout the war and used by all of the Allied forces. It normally mounted a 75 mm main gun, a 50 cal. heavy machine gun and a pair of 30 cal. machine guns, with crew of five. Later models had heavier main weapons. (RJP)

Today on display at Arromanches, these are some sections from the floating roadways that connected the Mulberry harbours to the shore. (RJP)

British heavy Churchill tank. This being a Hobart 'funny' model known as a Crocodile, it ejected flames from an especially adapted nozzle. (RJP)

A Higgins boat. Thousands
of these landing craft in
numerous variations provided
the means to land soldiers,
vehicles and weapons onto
target beaches. (RJP)

Off the Normandy coast at
Arromanches, the remains of
the massive concrete Mulberry
units that were floated across
the English Channel to provide
a makeshift portable harbour
for the Normandy operation
can still be seen. (RJP)

Bits and pieces of the Mulberry
harbours still litter the beach
and surf at
Arromanches. (RJP)

A G-4 Waco glider used to carry American airborne soldiers behind Utah Beach the night before the actual Utah Beach assault. It held up to thirteen fully equipped soldiers, or a small vehicle (a Jeep) or heavy weapon. Over 300 Wacos were employed behind Utah. They were usually towed by the C-47 Skytrain. (US Army)

An American M-10 tank destroyer. Using a basic M-4 Sherman tank carriage, it usually featured a 3-inch main gun mounted on a turret, and a 50 cal. machine gun. (RJP)

One of the many LSTs that provided immediate reinforcements of armour, equipment and supplies. These flat-bottomed vessels literally beached themselves and would then open their huge front doors and off-loading ramp. (NARA)

Above left: One of Hobart's Funnies, a flail tank designed to destroy mines and barbed wire. (LOC)

Above right: Yankee ingenuity. American soldiers devised fork-like iron prongs that would be attached to their tanks in order to penetrate the bushy French Bocage. (LOC)

Above left: The Mulberry portable harbour and floating roadway at the British Sword Beach. The American Mulberry at Omaha was destroyed during the 'Great Storm' of 19–21 June. (US Navy)

Above right: A Mulberry harbour. An aerial view of the breakwater and portable Mulberry dock with numerous transport ships waiting to unload. (US Navy)

Chapter 7

Naval Bombardment

I had never heard or seen a battleship firing a salvo … when they fired, it felt as though our landing craft lifted clean out of the water, such was the suction as the huge shells travelled overhead.

Sgt John DeVink, as his landing craft headed toward Utah Beach

The preliminary American naval bombardment at Utah Beach was conducted by an array of craft. It included one older battleship (USS *Nevada*) and several cruisers (USS *Quincy* and *Tuscaloosa* and the British HMS *Black Prince*), along with a hybrid gunboat (a flat-bottomed monitor – HMS *Erebus*) that carried two large 15-inch guns, and over a dozen destroyers. There were, of course, dozens of smaller ships, both transport and fighting craft, to support and reinforce the beachhead once it was established. The naval armada sailing to reach all five of the beaches, Operation Neptune, was under the overall command of the British Admiral Sir Bertram Ramsey. The American sector of western beaches, Omaha and Utah, was directed by American Admiral Alan Kirk, while the Utah operation was under US Admiral Don Moon. The opening phase would begin at dawn's first light, commencing with concentrated counter-battery fire intended to silence the German gun emplacements along Utah Beach. Counter-battery fire would hopefully mop up any threatening guns that were left undestroyed by the aircraft bombing missions of the previous few weeks. There were several known German big gun artillery positions, of various strength and deposition, and the initial naval gunfire would target these. The bombardment would continue to fire on designated targets even if they had previously been ruled as out of action. Such was the level of saturation earmarked in concentrated intensity to fully ensure the destruction of any guns and their attendant defensive structures.

At midnight on 6 June, the initial naval component of minesweepers sailed across the English Channel to begin sweeping the five coastal regions that would be used as the landing area for the 150,000 soldiers following in their transports. The minesweepers had two major tasks: sweep the English Channel passages for the forthcoming transports, and clear areas near the beach to allow the heavy bombardment and gunboat units to operate. The minesweepers encountered virtually no enemy activity and were able to complete their operation in time for the arrival of the warships that would commence the shore bombardment preceding the actual landings. Twenty minutes before the landings, the naval bombardment shifted to the actual beach emplacements in an attempt to destroy anti-tank guns, the dreaded German 88 mms, and any remaining dug-in machine-gun positions, pillboxes and bunkers. Spotting for the bombardment units was carried out by the RAF using radio communication. Limited in their range, the fighters flew in sequenced patterns in order to maintain continuous observation of the targets.

At 05:00, an hour ahead of the scheduled landings, the German defenders at Utah Beach spotted two American destroyers and several minesweepers off the beach and opened fire. The British cruiser *Black Prince* then began returning fire and the bombardment was on. As the invading landing craft left their transports and slowly approached the beaches, the bombardment lifted from firing on the beach proper to begin concentrating on the rear echelon areas behind the beaches and flanks, destroying or pinning down any would-be reinforcement units. In the interlude, as the initial naval bombardment ended, and as the landing craft made their journey to the shore, the air bombardment began again, this time with B-26 Marauder medium bombers. Flying parallel to the beach, the low-flying aircraft delivered nearly 5,000 bombs to pin down the German defenders that had survived the opening naval barrage. Utah Beach naval destroyers and escorts then provided a smokescreen to cover the oncoming Higgins landing craft with their assaulting troops. Unlike neighbouring Omaha Beach, both the air and naval bombardment at Utah Beach were extremely effective.

The battleship USS *Nevada*. Her heavy 14-inch guns provided pre-invasion bombardment at Utah Beach. (US Navy)

HMS *Erebus* was a big gun monitor (with two 15-inch guns) used to help pulverize the German defenses on Utah Beach the morning of D-Day. She proved very effective at off-shore bombardment. (LOC)

Big 14-inch guns from the battleship USS *Nevada* firing on Utah Beach. (US Navy)

Admiral Don Moon, commander of American naval forces for Utah Beach on D-Day. (US Navy)

The destroyer USS *Hobson*, which was one of many Allied destroyers that provided close-in gunfire onto beach positions and bunkers. This was very dangerous work in shallow off-shore conditions; at Utah Beach on D-Day, *Hobson*'s near-neighbour and sister ship, the destroyer USS *Corry*, struck a mine and was blown in half. This was the highest naval loss of life on D-Day. (US Navy)

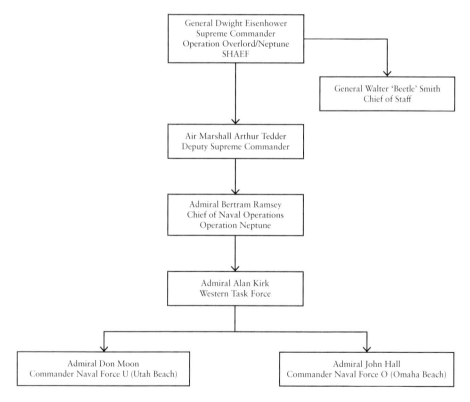

Operation Neptune and the naval command structure for crossing the English Channel and landing on the two American beaches, Utah and Omaha.

Chapter 8

Air Power

[On D-Day] there isn't going to be any German air force!
  Major General Elwood 'Pete' Quesada (advocate and chief of tactical air support for
    Overlord) in response to Major General J. Lawton 'Lightning Joe' Collins inquiring
    how the Allies would prevent the German air forces from destroying the D-Day landing

The might of Allied air dominance on D-Day was so great that not a single Allied airplane was shot down by enemy aircraft. Of the 113 Allied planes that were lost, all were brought down by anti-aircraft fire, as the German Luftwaffe was unable to mount any type of defence. In fact, the Germans had virtually no air force remaining with which to even attempt a defence. On D-Day alone, the Allies employed nearly 3,500 heavy bombers, 1,600 medium bombers and over 5,400 fighters to combat an almost empty catalogue of German combat aircraft.[7] These planes delivered punishing ground support for the five invasion beaches, knocking out bunkers, pillboxes and encased gun revetments. More important, however, were the tactical attacks on the rear areas of roads, rails and junctions behind the enemy lines that prevented any movement of German mobile reinforcements. The dreaded Panzer armoured divisions never left their stand-to positions, believing all along that the Allied attack at Normandy was only a feint and that the real attack was to come elsewhere. Assuming these Panzer divisions had ventured into action, it is more than conceivable that they would have been decimated by the lethal tactical air arm of the Allies. As it was, the Panzers survived in reserve to fight another day.

As suffocating as the Allied air assault was on D-Day, the real work of the air command had been accomplished months in advance. Eisenhower and the SHAEF commanders had been given full operational priority for air power to serve the ongoing ruse that Calais was the main point of attack, while disguising the intended Normandy location. This called for the obliteration of every access road and rail line that could provide any support for the coastal defences. The ratio, though, was two to one, with Normandy bombardment receiving only one-third, compared to the other two-thirds allotted to the other potential targets including Calais. Even with Normandy's diminished ratio, no road or railway, junction or staging area would be neglected for repeated pounding by the air forces. So thorough were air raids that, by late May 1944, very few targets remained, and nothing could safely move in the daylight on the open road or rail routes – it would be suicidal. At the same time, the German Luftwaffe had been all but destroyed, either on the ground or by being drawn into the air for combat. By late spring 1944, the skies had been cleared of German warplanes, and there was no thought of the Luftwaffe replacing either the planes or the ground crews. The fact was that the veteran pilot crews had been eliminated before the availability of more aircraft. The only remaining pilots and aircrews were fresh, green replacements with little or no training. Lacking experience and hopelessly outnumbered, these raw recruits were easy pickings for the Allied air command.

Since the Allies had already seized control of the skies, threatening any movement over the roads, rails and junction depots of France, a decision was made early in 1944 concerning the pre-invasion air assault on French civilians. As the air raids began in earnest, the remaining question to consider was what to do about these French civilians who would be in harm's way. The unfortunate answer was to accept the consequences in order to gain the essential triumph. As it turned out, French civilians suffered over 15,000 casualties in and around the German transport and staging areas. Such was the tragic cost in order to remove the Nazi occupation of France. So concerned were the Allies about the impending threat to the French civilian population that millions of leaflets were dropped over western France, defining and explaining the necessity for the bombing of French civilian targets. Beginning in March 1944, 130 million leaflets were distributed from Allied aircraft flying over France, and thereafter over 100 million each month leading up to D-Day.[8] Tragically, Allied bombing missions over France killed more than 53,000 French civilians during the entirety of the war, while injuring over 70,000. This compares to over 40,000 British civilians killed during the German Blitz of 1940–41, with an additional 20,000 killed during the rest of the war.[9] Certainly the massive pre-invasion bombing campaign was required, and just as certainly there were going to be French civilian casualties. The issue was debated in the highest SHAEF circles, but in March 1944 Eisenhower came down firmly with the decision to use heavy and continuous bombing raids on the rail system, marshalling yards and any and all strategic targets before and during the invasion of France.[10] There would, of course, also be collateral damage and casualties due to bad weather, mission error and the nature of the target location in urban areas, but that risk would have to be accepted.

Tolerance of French civilian casualties and the ensuing political ramifications with an occupied ally was repeatedly debated, but again, the decision hinged on the goal of completely bottling up the capacity for German reinforcement before, during and after the invasion. For the six-month pre-invasion campaign, seventy-six key locations were identified on the French railway network alone. Estimates ranged from RAF Bomber Command's prediction of 80,000–160,000 French casualties to a survey conducted by British scientific advisor Solly Zuckerman that 12,000 would be killed and 6,000 would be seriously injured.[11] Zuckerman and Eisenhower's own Chief of Allied Expeditionary Air Forces for the invasion, Trafford Leigh-Mallory, had developed what was known as the Transportation Plan. Its goal was to reduce the threat of reinforcing German units by systematically destroying the rail system leading west out of Paris. Although the Transportation Plan was potentially effective for every aspect of the tactical program, it also endangered large numbers of French civilians. Prime Minister Winston Churchill espoused deep reservations about the campaign, but reluctantly gave his approval due to the necessity of doing everything possible to ensure success of the invasion. Casualty figures would be recorded and reported by French resistance fighters and through the month of April 1944, the rate of 1,000 dead per month was in line with the more conservative predictions. However, by May 1944 it was clear that a more concentrated level of bombardment would be required, and at Roosevelt's insistence, Churchill gave his final approval and the unrestricted campaign assumed a more pronounced focus.[12]

The Transportation Plan for the air campaign over France then began in earnest, as over 71,000 tons of bombs were dropped on French transportation targets alone.[13] The damage effectively devastated German transport of supplies and equipment, but as feared, much of this explosive power was off the mark and nowhere near the pre-determined targets. The result became decidedly more costly in French civilian casualties: from 700 killed in March to 5,000 in April, and then a leap to 9,800 and 9,500 in May and June respectively. This meant over 25,000 killed during the six months leading up to the invasion – or more than double the conservative estimates. However, the overall effect was critical in preventing the movement of German troops, equipment and supplies.[14]

Arguments and disagreements continued between the various Allied air groups over the use and practicality of using heavy bombers versus lighter and faster fighter-bombers for the air interdiction campaign over France. Eisenhower threatened to resign his post unless the issue was resolved, calling upon Marshall in Washington to finally settle the question. Marshall responded and ordered that the Overlord mission would hold precedent through the spring and until the invasion was completed.[15] It was true that the heavy bombers were ill-suited for the exceedingly difficult mission of precision interdiction, even with their high capacity for tonnage of saturation bombing. Only partially successful through early spring, the turning point came when the decision was reached to employ the overwhelming Allied strength of 9,000 fighters in the fighter-bomber interdiction role. Turned loose in late March, for the next two months the fighter-bombers of the US 9th Air Force did what the big bombers could not do. Particularly useful was the destruction of railway repair sheds, preventing the repair of locomotives and rail carriages. Railway bridges over the rivers west of Paris were nearly impossible for the higher altitude heavies to accurately hit but were extremely vulnerable to the low-flying fighters such as the P-47 Thunderbolt. The havoc created by these tactics, coupled with the strafing of trains in movement, rail yards, junctions and staging areas, made train travel a nightmare for the Germans and near certain death for anyone who attempted to travel by road or rail during the day. By D-Day, virtually no daytime rail or road traffic was even being attempted, let alone succeeding. A secondary benefit was the continued annihilation of the German Luftwaffe, whether parked on runways or in the air attempting to offer a feeble challenge to the Allied interdiction program. In short, it became a stunning success.[16]

D-DAY

On D-Day itself, the Allies placed over 10,000 aircraft into the air with virtually no interference from the Luftwaffe. Even if the Allied chiefs were not in total agreement over method and means, there was no question as to the need and the ability of the air arm to dominate the skies over the English Channel and all of western France. D-Day's bombing mission for the air forces was conducted in stages, in concert with and similar to the naval bombardment. The first phase of the air action used heavy bombers targeting specifically defined targets of heavily reinforced concrete bunkers and the rear-area roads leading into the target areas. What was not attacked using heavy bombs was the actual beach itself. This was to prevent the bombing action from severely cratering the beach and adding to the obstacles for arriving armoured units. These units needed to manoeuver on the beach in support and then begin to penetrate beyond and into the interior. This point had been debated by the commanders, who weighed the value of bombing the immediate objective – the beach – as opposed to leaving the beach clear for the oncoming armoured vehicles to pierce the German front line. Severe cratering would also impede incoming waves of reinforcements and the necessary mass of supplies and reinforcement vehicles to follow. Controversial as it was, after much discussion it was decided to leave the actual beach area intact and concentrate the air attacks to the rear area or on specified targets.

Another concern was collateral harm to the attacking forces. Weather dictated precision, and bad weather limited the degree of precision and greatly increased the risk of lethal 'friendly fire' on their own troops. Without the guarantee of clear weather, and coupled with the close proximity to the invading assault groups, there was fear that bombing and strafing too close to the shoreline would pose a far greater risk of lethal friendly fire. The weather on D-Day was cloudy and, in this sense, the more conservative decision was probably correct. However, there was no fall-back plan for the use of heavy and medium bombers at low altitude under the cloud cover, and when the overcast conditions interfered, the use of this alternative on the actual shore front was completely denied. Unlike the later Pacific island invasion operations, there was no available aircraft carrier support or communications network to call in tactical air strikes as needed. This use of a combined naval, air, ground and communication network was in its infancy, and it was never part of the Atlantic calculation as it was in the Pacific theatre.

The use of heavy bombers was attempted in several instances for tactical deployment throughout the Normandy campaign but found wanting. Lack of sufficient training, the inaccuracy of the weapon systems for specific tactical targets as opposed to strategic area targets, and weather factors all limited the suitability of strategic heavy bombers to properly conduct tactical missions. This had been pointed out to Eisenhower and the Allied high command by both British and American air commanders, but they were overruled by the necessity for complete commitment to the invasion's success. However, the larger and greater use of fighters and medium bombers proved more and more effective as the campaign developed, and they gradually became accepted as essential to the concept of mixed weapons warfare. On Utah Beach and the other four assault beaches, tactical air support was limited to providing umbrella air protection over the invading fleet and its vast array of ships, and to providing cover for the bombers flying deeper over France. Unlike neighbouring Omaha Beach, Utah Beach would receive some benefit from fighter-bomber action immediately ahead of the actual invasion day landing. 360 B-26 Marauder medium bombers of the 9th Air Force were able to inflict significant damage to German beach positions just prior to the assault force landings.

Following D-Day, as the Normandy campaign evolved over the following months, the growing recognition and proficiency of tactical air support would lead to devastating effects on retreating German formations, and in particular the violent rout of the retreating German armies at the Falaise Pocket in late July as the Allies finally succeeded in breaking out of the Normandy front.

Seen at a recent American air show, this American P- 51 Mustang fighter was used to provide umbrella air cover over the D-Day landings. (RJP)

A B-26 Marauder twin-engine medium bomber. 360 Marauders successfully pounded German positions along Utah Beach just ahead of the arriving assault team in a superb display of tactical interdiction – a feature that was sadly missing at nearby Omaha Beach. (US Army)

Churchill and Eisenhower generally got along well, occasional differences of opinion notwithstanding, and shared an excellent relationship. One major disagreement concerned the heavy bombing of French rail lines and railyards preceding D-Day. Churchill feared a heavy toll of French civilian casualties, while the Overlord high command demanded the complete severing of the German ability to reinforce Normandy. Roosevelt interceded and the Transportation Plan went ahead to great success, although so too did Churchill's feared civilian casualties. (US Army)

A British Spitfire fighter at a recent American air show. These and other Allied fighters provided umbrella air cover for the invasion on D-Day. (RJP)

An American B-17 heavy bomber at a recent American air show. It was part of the Transportation Plan to destroy the French railway system prior to D-Day. (RJP)

A-20 Havocs, typical medium bombers, over a French railyard while destroying and blocking German military transportation prior to D-Day. (NARA)

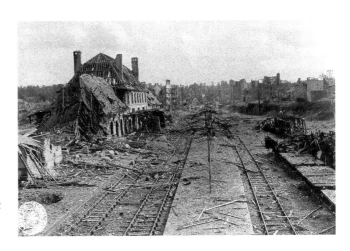

The devastation of French railyards, as carried out through the controversial Transportation Plan to disrupt German operations prior to D-Day. (NARA)

An American P-47 Thunderbolt fighter, used for effective and devastating low-level interdiction of French rail lines and umbrella air cover during D-Day. (US Army)

General Pete Quesada, commander of American fighter forces during the Normandy campaign. It was Quesada who famously, and correctly, predicted that 'there would be no German Air Force' to oppose the Allies on D-Day. (US Army)

Chapter 9

The Airborne Assault is Launched

O.K. We'll go.

> Allied Supreme Commander General Dwight Eisenhower's decision
> to commence the Overlord operation in spite of ominous weather that
> had already delayed the invasion by one day.

The unpredictable and frequently violent weather of the English Channel had always been the unknown 'Joker' in the deck of all Overlord planning. The window of available invasion dates was dictated by tide, moonlit nights and, ultimately, the weather. Already postponed one day due to the frightful storms hovering over north-western Europe, the chance opening of a narrow gap of modestly 'fair' weather signalled the opportunity for Eisenhower to launch the invasion of France. The Utah Beach invasion was opened by a daring and dramatic airborne assault on the night of 5/6 June as American invaders descended by the thousands from the sky in the form of paratroopers or passengers aboard towed gliders, along with the British airborne drops behind the beach designated 'Sword'. The Allies began arriving in force to invade and liberate occupied France.

The south-western flank of the D-Day invasion was the responsibility of the Utah Beach sector near the neck of the Cotentin Peninsula. Sword Beach, on the opposite north-eastern edge, became the target of the British. Both of these flanks needed to be tightly sealed to ensure that the Germans would not be able to outflank the invaders. The central beaches, Omaha, Gold, and Juno, held the centre and would attempt to thrust forward. In order to ensure this flank protection, it was decided to insert airborne forces behind Utah and Sword Beaches the night before the morning invasion. One British airborne division was assigned to drop behind Sword Beach and two American airborne divisions were placed behind Utah Beach. It was the biggest airborne operation of the war up until that time.

Over 13,000 American paratroopers of the 82nd and 101st Airborne Divisions were either carried by towed glider aircraft or dropped from C-47 Dakota transports during the night of 5/6 June. They immediately seized and secured strategic roads, intersections and bridges in order to prevent the Germans from bringing up reinforcements at the outset of the following day's invasion. They then sought to link up with the assaulting infantry to further secure the Utah Beach zone and begin to penetrate into the French interior. On Sword Beach, the British 6th Airborne Division did the same. The British operation was completely successful and was accomplished with minimum casualties while securing the Orne River bridges. The Americans, while also successful, encountered problems of missed drop sites, poor timing and other navigational frustrations. The American problems stemmed from fog, confusion over drop points and poor navigation. In fact, some paratroopers were even mistakenly dropped into the English Channel.[17] There was also a lack of training on the part of pilots and air crews for the type of night-time flying required to properly release paratroopers.[18]

Both British and American airborne forces arrived either by parachute or as part of a fleet of gliders that were able to carry larger loads and heavier equipment and deliver more men to a site. The G-4 Waco glider proved to be extremely practical and beneficial in the early stages of the invasion, when surprise and long reach behind enemy lines were critical. With its capacity for heavy loads, relative durability and hinged front hatch allowing ease of loading and abundance in service, it was the main glider resource for the American airborne divisions during the D-Day invasions. 300 Wacos were employed behind Utah Beach for the initial D-Day invasion. Of the two initial glider groups, one-third were lost due to accidents and enemy gunfire, and 100 more were sent over immediately following the first day's invasion. The second day deployments in daylight allowed for almost 100 per cent success with few injuries.[19]

All gliders required a smooth landing field and the vision to locate it – there could be no turning back once they dropped altitude. The British used the larger Horsa glider, with a capacity for up to twenty-five soldiers or extra tonnage and equipment. Gliders would be towed by the C-47 Skytrain/Dakota, at around 125 mph and, when within range of its objective, would be released to land in a pasture or field. For this reason, Field Marshal Rommel had the Germans scatter the landscape with upright log poles, termed 'asparagus', into the pastures and open fields throughout the French countryside to wreck any would-be glider landings. They often worked to lethal effect. Glider pilots were not necessarily pilots in an air corps sense, but non-commissioned officers who, upon landing, immediately took up weapons and fought as infantry.[20]

Paratrooper drops were led by 'pathfinder units', who would then guide the following C-47s into the correct target zones – the glider landings came later. Unfortunately, due to bad weather and fog, limited training and inadequate navigational equipment and operation, many of the pathfinder units went off course. This led to many of the trailing C-47s also going off course and only one of the eighteen pathfinder units arrived at the correct drop zone.[21] Released paratroopers then floated to unknown destinations. The night-time glider landings had mixed results, but mishaps involving the fragile gliders were usually disastrous. Again, due to navigational difficulties, many glider landings, even when safely conducted, were off target, sometimes by many miles. In one crash landing, the deputy commander of the 101st Airborne Division, Brigadier General Donald Pratt, was killed. Those gliders that successfully landed were often damaged to such an extent that they were unfit to be used again – they were basically one-time-only aircraft. However, it was an optional method to both increase the number of paratroopers landed and deliver the essential heavier equipment required for the mission, and many successfully fulfilled their target goals.

The Douglas C-47 Skytrain/Dakota was the mainstay of the Allied air transport effort. Its versatility, durability and handling made it legendary as it flew every sort of transport mission during the Second World War. With more than 10,000 produced, the C-47 fought in every theatre of the Second World War. The C-47 also delivered British paratroopers on the far eastern flank behind the British Sword Beach. Over 900 C-47s were used the night before D-Day, with seventeen being shot down by anti-aircraft fire.

As dawn approached behind the Utah Beach assault zone, the two airborne divisions attempted to prevent the Germans from reinforcing their comrades defending the beaches, then moved on in an effort to link up with their own assault units. Fanning out, the airborne units also provided an immediate shield for the right (western) flank of the invasion and secured a springboard to seal off the Cotentin Peninsula. The move into the Cotentin Peninsula would be a step toward seizing the important port of Cherbourg on the western tip. The airborne units, delivered by the C-47 in its great numbers, were the instruments used to place those soldiers in that essential tactical position.

Above left: American paratroopers boarding a C-47 the evening before D-Day. (US Army)

Above right: General Dwight Eisenhower with American airborne soldiers the day before D-Day. (US Army Signal Corps)

C-47 pilots being briefed before their missions towing gliders or delivering paratroopers and equipment behind Utah Beach.

A small, mobile howitzer, capable of being delivered by Waco glider. (RJP)

Loading an American C-47 transport with paratroopers to begin the assault behind Utah Beach. (US Army)

A G-4 Waco glider on display at the Airborne Museum in Sainte-Mère-Église. (RJP)

The nose of the G-4 Waco was hinged for the easy loading of heavy equipment or personnel. In this photo the glider carries a small howitzer. (US Army)

A fully loaded Waco glider ready to cross the English Channel, and deliver its contingent of airborne troops behind Utah Beach. The Allies enjoyed total air superiority for the Normandy operation. (US Navy)

Chapter 10

D-Day Utah
Beach Airborne Assault

The plan for getting the troops to the drop zones in Normandy was the most complex and ambitions mission we had ever faced.
  Lieutenant Roger Airgood, American C-47 pilot flying at night behind Utah Beach

The C-47 pilots had been trained to fly transports as opposed to combat missions. The flight across the English Channel demanded an entirely different set of aviation responsibilities: dropping paratroopers while flying into a heavily defended combat zone, and flying in formation at night, another set of tasks for which most C-47 Dakota pilots had not been trained. Once over France, and while flying at a slower than top speed to drop the paratroopers (the C-47's top speed was less than 250 mph), the air armada met German resistance in the form of anti-aircraft flak. Combat flying, even in high-performance airplanes, was a dangerous and hair-raising enterprise for the most experienced combat pilots, let alone these neophytes in slow-moving transports.

C-47 pilots were worried for many other reasons, all very real and dangerous. Bad weather, flying in disciplined formations, night flying that relied on keying in on difficult navigational signals, flak from the Germans, and the mission itself – dropping off paratroopers and returning to base as opposed to landing passengers or supplies and equipment at a designated destination – all presented new and perilous challenges. The drops had to be conducted over the assigned targets if the paratroopers were to have any hope of regrouping and performing their operations. Since the number of C-47s crossing the Channel was so great, the chance of mid-air collisions was a major danger. These pilots were not trained for mass formation operations.

The formation was aligned in a pattern of 'V's within a greater V that stretched 300 miles across the night sky. The Vs were nine planes wide and all radio contact was forbidden; it was strictly navigation by line of sight, point to point, from various electronic and visual signals through line-of-sight beacon observation. Only 1,000 feet separated the groups in altitude levels, and the lowest group skimmed the English Channel at only 500 feet in order to avoid German radar and observation. When the jump signal was given, the paratroopers plunged into the night sky and for several minutes were completely exposed to German ground fire, assuming the Germans saw them and realised what they were seeing. Private William True of the 506th expressed perfectly what many experienced as they glided to earth: 'Unbelievable! ... that there were people down there shooting at me! Trying to kill Bill True!'[22]

Many of the release jump points were in the wrong area, were poorly timed and had planes going either too fast or flying too low, as this was not only the first combat jump for most of the troopers, but also the first jump release for most of the C-47 pilots. Private John Taylor stepped out of his C-47 and realized immediately that they were very, very low: 'We don't need a parachute for this; all we need is a step ladder'. And as Private John Fitzgerald floated downward and watched bullets 'rip through my chute',

> I was mesmerised by the scene around me. Every colour of the rainbow was flashing through the sky. Equipment bundles attached to chutes that did not fully open came hurtling past me, helmets that had been ripped off by the opening shock, troopers floated past. Below me, figures were running in all directions. I thought, Christ, I'm going to land right in the middle of a bunch of Germans! My chute floated into the branches of an apple tree in full bloom and added a strange scent to this improbable scene ... and it was the Germans who it turned out were running for cover ... I felt a strange surge of elation: I was alive![23]

In fog, darkness and confusion, deep in enemy territory, the paratroopers were scattered over an area covering some 50 square miles. Some individuals were able to meet, form groups and carry on; others wandered about alone, tensely afraid and hopelessly lost; still others were identified, captured or shot and killed. Ironically, however, the wide dispersal led the Germans to believe that the airborne landing was much larger than it was. The complete chaos that ensued prevented any recognition of where the focal point of the landing was. This lack of a singular focus point also encouraged the German commanders to maintain their belief in the Normandy operation as a feint – again playing into the Allies' desire for deception and preventing the Germans from launching a concentrated alarm and calling for reinforcement. To further confuse the Germans, the American airborne thought to drop squads of 'dummy' paratroopers to give the illusion of greater numbers and wrong locations, as well as to draw off German patrols and provoke gunfire which would reveal their positions. This proved to be an extraordinarily successful deception.

Three hours after the initial parachute drop, the gliders began to arrive with their heavier manpower and equipment loads. The attempted landings into dark and unknown conditions led to numerous crash landings. Miraculously, many gliders survived the anti-aircraft fire and, under extremely difficult conditions, were able to find a suitable field and complete a reasonably safe landing.

Paratrooper Private Fitzgerald watched the gliders come in and was astonished by the quiet sound they emitted as they proceeded to crash in every direction:

... a series of swishing noises ... of sounds ... tearing of branches and trees followed by loud crashes and intermittent screams. The gliders were coming in rapidly, one after the other, from all different directions. Many overshot the field and landed in the surrounding woods, while others crashed into nearby farmhouses and stone walls ... In a moment the field was complete chaos. Equipment broke away and catapulted as it hit the ground, ploughing up huge mounds of earth. Bodies and bundles were thrown all along the length of the field. Some of the glider troopers were impaled by the splintering wood of the fragile plywood gliders.[24]

Before D-Day, glider casualties had been predicted by the Allies to go as high as 70 per cent.[25] Even though the rate of loss for men and equipment approached a very high level of 20 per cent, it provided important elements of reinforcements, equipment and especially the essential anti-tank guns and jeeps.

While meaningful numbers of soldiers aimlessly roamed the French countryside, many troopers did link up, meet and coalesce. By dawn, the groups that had organised were able to identify several objectives and destroy German bunkers and pillboxes while seizing road intersections to prevent German reinforcements from interfering with the Utah Beach landing that was now underway. The town of Sainte-Mère-Église became the first French town to be captured in the D-Day offensive. Eventually, the paratroopers merged with the invading infantry while also blocking and cutting off the German connection to the Cotentin Peninsula and the ability to reinforce that area with its all-important port of Cherbourg.

The American airborne assault was a success.

A crashed and flipped over American glider with its mortal contents, testament to the disaster. (LOC)

Right and below: Sainte-Mère-Église. Due to bad weather, bad navigation and bad luck, many paratroopers of the American airborne landed in surprising locations and none was more surprised than Private John Steele. Steele ended up on the roof of the church in the center of town. Later taken prisoner, he escaped and rejoined his unit and is commemorated annually with a parachute and manikin draped down across the steeple. (RJP)

Above left: German soldiers inspecting an American glider that successfully landed and unloaded its cargo. Clearly visible is the open nose section for ease of unloading. (NARA)

Above right: A squadron of gliders preparing to land in an open field in Normandy. Many pastures and fields were studded with timber poles ('Rommel's asparagus') to prevent glider landing. This is probably on D-Day +1, when reinforcing airborne units were sent across the Channel in clearer daylight conditions. (LOC)

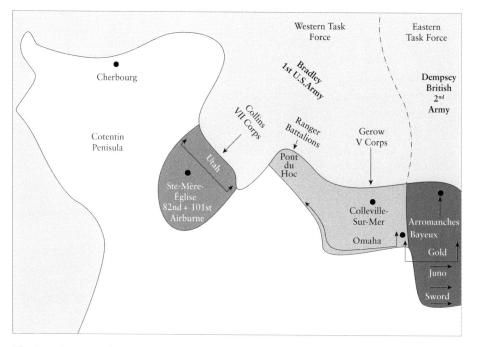

The American assault teams were assigned the western Normandy beaches, codenamed Utah and Omaha.

Chapter 11

D-Day Utah Beach Invasion

We have landed in the wrong place, but we will start the war from right here.
General Theodore Roosevelt Jnr. upon arriving at Utah Beach after his invading
units were pushed off course by the strong ocean surf.

Preceded by an effective naval bombardment and followed with an aerial attack by
300 low-level medium bombers to soften up beach defences, the Utah Beach assault
gained traction right from the start. Unlike the insufficient naval bombardment
and the sadly deficient aerial operation at Omaha Beach, the Utah Beach offensive
was accurate, smothering and on time. In contrast to the ongoing potential disaster
at Omaha Beach, the Utah invasion was not only successful in achieving its early
objectives, but was able to deliver 21,000 soldiers of the 4th Infantry Division and the
70th Tank Battalion to the beach, while suffering only limited casualties. There were
perhaps fewer than 700 casualties recorded at the Utah Beach landings, although
more than three times that number were incurred during the night-time airborne
drops of paratroopers and glider landings, as a total of 2,500 of 14,000 paratroopers
arriving by parachute and glider fell victim to either accidents or German gunfire.

German positions at Utah were weak, undermanned and serviced by second-line
troops – often from regiments recruited from the occupied countries. It was an area
that the Germans had neglected to strongly defend and that Rommel had recently and
belatedly attempted to bolster with mines, obstacles and increased troop dispositions.
Rommel was short of any and all soldiers, resources and, most importantly, time.
His attempt to protect Hitler's Fortress Europe with an Atlantic Wall was a virtual
impossibility given the length of European shoreline to guard and the already thinly
stretched manpower and resources he had available. Manpower was at a premium
and troops that were re-equipping, along with second-line and under-strength units,
were often pressed into service to build the defensive structures and obstacles along
the shores and beaches of western France, Belgium and Holland.

Following the airborne drop and naval and aerial bombardments, the initial
Utah Beach assault was carried out in four waves. The first wave was the 70th Tank

Battalion, composed of thirty-two tanks. Due to the high surf and winds, they were dropped off from their landing craft 1,500 yards from shore, much closer than the originally planned 5,000 yards. Only four tanks or tank-carrying landing craft were lost to the sea and German gunfire; this enabled twenty-eight tanks to successfully make it to shore in support of the arriving infantry. This was a marked difference from the frustrations and failures going on simultaneously at Omaha Beach, where tanks were swamped in large numbers, leaving the unsupported infantry to surmount substantially longer beach distances, unescorted and lacking adequate firepower to accomplish their objectives.

The second wave was comprised of members of the 8th Infantry Regiment and units of engineers and combat demolition teams, who were to clear obstacles and mines for the next two oncoming waves of assaulting forces. These groups of engineers took heavy casualties as they went about their dangerous work while under German fire. However, within an hour the beach had been seized and both infantry and armoured forces were pushing inland to their assigned objectives and the planned link-up with the airborne divisions.

Utah Beach was under the direct command of VII Corps commander General Joseph ('Lightning Joe') Lawton Collins, a veteran of several Pacific campaigns against the Japanese. Collins was brought to the European theatre for his experience in amphibious assaults and a well-earned reputation for aggressive action. His assignment at Utah was to take the beach, link up with the airborne element, cut off the Cotentin Peninsula and begin the advance toward the seizure of the important port of Cherbourg.

Besides encountering weak and confused German resistance, the Allies enjoyed some other benefits of unexpected good fortune. Being the most westerly and exposed beach, Utah Beach possessed the strongest ocean currents for the landing craft to contend with. The strong current, a virtually featureless landscape and visibility shrouded by gun smoke only added to the difficulty for the landing craft attempting to locate and navigate to their designated beach area. Swept off course, the landing craft ended up over a mile to the east of their assigned targets. In a quick-thinking response, the assaulting troops rapidly implemented an alternative plan, remaining where they were and securing their objectives with minimal loss of life. The oncoming arrival of additional armour and infantry, even though landing in the wrong area, was rapidly adjusted, reorganised and successfully redeployed for the new location. The leadership and cool recognition of the situation, followed by the appropriate and effective reaction to the circumstances, was carried out by the commanders on the beach, including fifty-six-year-old Theodore Roosevelt Jnr, the assistant commander of the 4th Division.

Brigadier General Theodore Roosevelt Jnr was the son of former US President Theodore Roosevelt. Theodore Junior had been wounded while fighting in the First World War as an officer with the 1st Infantry Division; for this he had received the Distinguished Service Cross. His brother, pilot Quentin Roosevelt, was killed in the

First World War during aerial combat. At the outbreak of the Second World War, Roosevelt re-entered the army and served in North Africa and Sicily with the 1st Division. Before the Normandy invasion, he was transferred to the 4th Infantry Division as second in command, where he insisted upon going ashore with the initial landing teams. He was at this time fifty-six years old, required a cane and suffered from several physical infirmities. He was the oldest US soldier to hit the beach at Utah, arriving with the first wave of assault troops.

After being swept a mile to the east from the intended landing area, and upon reaching the wrong site, Roosevelt consulted his map and famously proclaimed, 'We'll start the war from right here,' and proceeded to rally his troops to a successful operation. In fact, it had been most opportune to end up where they did, as this section of beach was much less stoutly defended than the proposed landing point. Roosevelt was seen directing troops throughout the day and was awarded the Congressional Medal of Honor for his visible and active participation.

There can be no denying Roosevelt's bravery and leadership in front of his troops; however, there is some discussion as to whether it was indeed his idea to remain there. Another source, Colonel James Van Fleet, commander of the 8th Infantry Regiment, later wrote, 'I made the decision. "Go straight inland," I ordered. "We've caught the enemy at a weak point, so let's take advantage of it."' According to Van Fleet, later a general and commanding officer during the Korean War, the error in landing zone due to the robust currents actually placed his regiment where he had originally recommended it be dropped, but the Navy had rejected the request due to the waters being too shallow. 'We faced an immediate and important decision, should we try to shift our entire landing force more than a mile down the beach, and follow our original plan? Or should we proceed across the causeway immediately opposite where we had landed?' With engineers and demolition teams already at work, the decision was made to establish their position where they had landed and press on from there.[26] The important point was the agreement by all parties and the positive result: less German resistance, greater opportunity for success in maintaining the beachhead and an immediate advance into the French interior.

Roosevelt was popular with his soldiers and always desired to be on or near the front line, close to his troops. He was forced to use a cane due to acute arthritis, endured a severe heart condition and died of a sudden heart attack less than six weeks later while in France. He is buried with his fellow troops at the American military cemetery, Colleville-sur-Mer, overlooking Omaha Beach. His younger brother Quentin, buried in France after his death in the First World War, was later re-interred beside him. Teddy Roosevelt Jnr's son, also named Quentin, wasn't far from his father, leading an assault unit on D-Day as an infantry captain at nearby Omaha Beach.

Although Utah escaped the heavy casualties of nearby Omaha Beach, the greater difficulty became moving off the beach and through the flooded conditions behind it, the Germans having flooded many square miles of countryside. This was done to prevent Allied airborne landings and to make difficult any exit path, even if the Allies were to successfully take the beach. Another problem after the Utah landings was linking up with the airborne units that were strewn over a wide area and completely detached. Once these two major challenges were dealt with, the drive up the Cotentin Peninsula could commence in earnest.

Rather than go around the floodwater, the decision was made to cross the waist-deep flooded fields and their dangerously slick muddy bottoms. Sergeant Clifford Sorenson of the 1st Battalion, having survived the Utah Beach landing, expressed his own apprehension and that of his fellow soldiers. 'I was so angry. The Navy had tried to drown me at the beach, and now the Army was trying to drown me in the flooded area. I was more mad at our side than I was at the Germans, because the Germans hadn't done anything to me yet.'[27] Several hours later, the battalion had crossed the flooded fields and began to link up with the scattered airborne units that had arrived from the opposite direction. At the same time, reinforcements of infantry, engineers and heavy equipment continued to unload along the newly captured Utah Beach.

Using the coordinated skill and combined efforts of several individual service units, including the US Army, Navy, Army Air Forces and Coast Guard, plus British contingents, the Utah Beach landing was a signature accomplishment of unified effort. In terms of rapidity and result, let alone the limited number of casualties for such a dangerous enterprise, the Utah Beach operation was a marvel of success. The difficult night-time landing of 14,000 paratroopers; the speed and efficiency of the 4th Division's landing, clearing, and seizure of its beach objectives; and the remarkable logistical triumph of landing over 20,000 soldiers and 1,700 vehicles in one day all seem incredible. Doing so in the face of the constant threat posed by Rommel's defences is even more astonishing. As witnessed at Omaha Beach, that threat could have turned tragic with the wrong chain of events. There were no guarantees.

Moving up the Cotentin Peninsula would prove a difficult task. The seizure of Cherbourg, achieved sixteen days later, was less than a complete success due to its demolition by the Germans before they surrendered. But Cherbourg would be serviceable by September and a valuable port of entry for future Allied supplies and reinforcements as troops fought their way across northern France. The Utah Beach flank also became the springboard for the encirclement of the Falaise Pocket, leading to the destruction of several German armoured and infantry divisions and allowing the breakout into the open French countryside by General George Patton's mobile armoured units, leading to the liberation of Paris.

All of the Allied beaches played an important role in the Operation Overlord invasion, and each had its own unique stories. In their stunning and rapid re-entry onto the western European continent, the Americans at Utah Beach proved just how determined, resourceful and well prepared the Allies were. The Normandy invasion presented a dramatic end to Hitler's belief in an invincible Atlantic Wall of Fortress Europe, and the next year's fighting would spell an end to Hitler's dream of a 'thousand-year Reich' dominating Europe and, perhaps, the world.

A fleet of LST transports heading for the Normandy beaches on D-Day. Supply and reinforcement began immediately following the securing of the beaches, sometimes while the fighting was still in progress. Several LSTs, a large, slow and valuable target, were destroyed. Once unloaded, LSTs became hospital ships for their return voyage to Britain. (US Navy)

Assaulting troops wading ashore at Utah Beach on 6 June 1944. The beach was quickly secured, reinforcing units began arriving immediately and the casualty list numbered less than 700 killed or wounded, unlike the 2,000 at neighboring Omaha Beach. (NARA)

A typical M-4 Sherman tank at Utah Beach today. Unlike at Omaha Beach, many of these tanks successfully made it ashore using their 'wading' attachments or 'DD' skirts to negotiate the surf. Conditions, of course, were entirely different at each location, from the state of the sea to German resistance. (RJP)

American soldiers preparing to unload at Utah Beach on D-Day. The congestion of vehicles and equipment going ashore can be seen nearer the beach. (US Coast Guard)

A specially adapted 'wading' Sherman tank being loaded prior to D-Day. These armoured vehicles performed very well in the low surf close to the shore of Utah Beach. (US Navy)

A fully loaded American LST transport with heavy equipment and vehicles crossing the English Channel to land on the Normandy beaches. Until a full-sized, functioning port was seized, LSTs and the lone Mulberry harbour delivered the bulk of equipment and supplies for the Normandy operation. (US Navy)

General Teddy Roosevelt Jnr, assistant commander of the 4th Division and an early arrival on Utah Beach. It was the fifty-six-year-old officer (the oldest to land on D-Day) who agreed with (or ordered) the decision to 'start the war right here' when his assaulting troops were carried a mile off course. It turned out to be a fortunate and tactically correct assessment. (US Army)

The grave of General Teddy Roosevelt Jnr, who died of a heart attack in July 1944 while serving with his troops in France. He is buried at the American Military Cemetery at Colleville-Sur-Mer, overlooking Omaha Beach. His grave is beside that of his brother Quentin, killed during the First World War. (RJP)

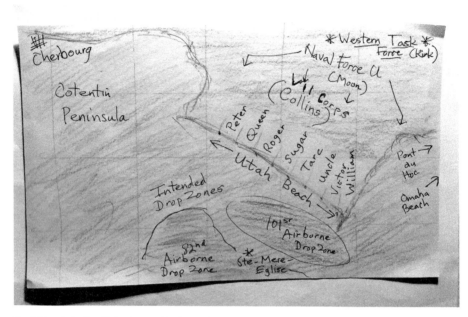

Utah Beach in detail. Utah would also include the American airborne assaults.

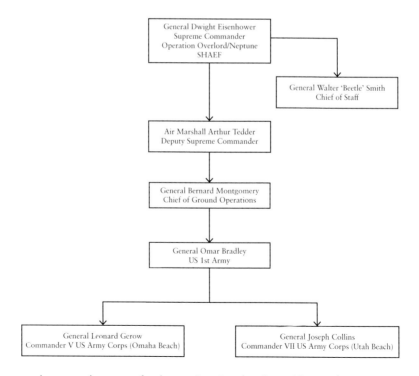

The ground command structure for the two American beaches at Normandy.

Chapter 12

Utah Beach Success

Remember, this is an invasion, not the creation of a fortified beachhead.
British Prime Minister Winston Churchill, on the true importance and
goal of the Overlord enterprise.

At Utah Beach, the major priorities were to secure the right flank of the overall invasion perimeter and provide an immediate connection to the Cotentin Peninsula for the drive to the north and the seizure of the important deep-water port of Cherbourg. Utah Beach was quickly captured on the morning of 6 June and both of these future objectives were eventually accomplished. However, it would be several days before the Allied forces could completely unite the five beaches, link up with their scattered airborne units and seal off the Cotentin Peninsula. This would then allow an advance up the peninsula to isolate Cherbourg and expedite the capture of the port. Meanwhile, maintaining control of the peninsula and denying Cherbourg to the Allies was also high on Field Marshal Erwin Rommel's list of priorities. Due to a confused and hastily assembled, but nonetheless determined, German defence, the Americans would require ten days to secure the peninsula and another two weeks to capture the besieged and broken city of Cherbourg. The original plan called for the capture of Cherbourg by D-Day +15, or two weeks after the initial landing, so the timetable fell behind by roughly one week as the Germans surrendered Cherbourg on D+21. By then the Cherbourg port facilities had been thoroughly sabotaged and destroyed by German demolitions. It would take a month of repairs to begin to restore the port's partial use and most of the summer to return it to full capacity. Cherbourg would be essential to provisioning and reinforcing the enormous Allied army and its logistical supply demands for the coming summer offensive. As a deep-water ocean port, Cherbourg would allow a direct unloading of transports from North America, rather than offloading in Britain, reloading in smaller vessels and crossing the English Channel to offload all over again in France. In the meantime, the surviving Mulberry port on the British Gold Beach, and the extensive use of the mammoth LST transports on the other beaches, would maintain the essential flow of supplies and reinforcements.

Once successfully ashore, it was a race between the Germans and the Allies to see who would reinforce their position the quickest. From their narrow beachheads, the Allies would disgorge prodigious quantities of resources, supplies and equipment while connecting the freshly captured beaches into a single front. In fact, the logjam on the beaches, with masses of continuously arriving men and equipment, was frequently a traffic bottleneck. Fortunately, the dominating Allied air cover would shield the ongoing supply effort that proved an endless puzzle to administer until more forward territory could be seized to broaden the initial position.

The Allied right flank, extending west and north from Utah Beach, would now attempt to become the springboard for the swing east to penetrate deep into the French countryside and drive north to surround the retreating German Army. The Germans still possessed the most intimidating army in Europe, an army that was rightly respected by the Allies. The Germans had had four years to fortify their defences with roughly fifty-eight divisions, including ten armoured Panzer divisions. During the assault, these units failed to effectively converge and defeat the Allies on the invasion beaches, as Rommel had feared, but they were now preparing to launch counterattacks to hurl the Allies off the beaches and back into the Channel. The successfully landed Allies were eager to immediately reinforce their initial wedge of six divisions, plus three airborne divisions, lodged along the narrow Normandy beachhead. Reinforcements would double the number of troops and resources within a week. But these forces, too, had to cross the stormy English Channel and disembark as the fleet of transports returned to Britain in an ongoing shuttle of re-supply.

THE BREAKOUT FROM UTAH AND THE VICTORY AT THE FALAISE POCKET

Once lodged into their beach enclave, and exactly as Rommel had predicted, the Allies were able to connect their beaches, deepen their holding position, reinforce their assault troops and expand their position, although the progress for more than a month was negligible. Once the Allies were established there was little the Germans could do except defend and counterattack. Although the Germans lacked any meaningful air support, the fighting was intense as they desperately sought to hold their position. This, however, was proving to be an advantage to the Allies as German defenders, troops and equipment alike, were being chewed up and ground down by the constant Allied pressure. Lacking sufficient reinforcements, the Germans were denied any opportunity for a consolidated counteroffensive.

On the eastern wing, Montgomery's British and Canadian forces were bogged down in the attempt to capture the important French junction town of Caen. Montgomery's relentless hammering finally advanced to seize Caen, while the western flank held by the Americans swung around to pivot and form a noose around the German positions, surrounding an entire German Army and nearly bagging the whole lot. Under the flanking sweep of the hard-driving General George Patton and his American 3rd

Army, much of the German defending forces – men, vehicles and equipment – were annihilated in the Falaise Pocket. Some Germans were able to escape, but their losses were heavy and their position was broken. The stunning victory provided the breach into north-western France and ignited a rapid advance, culminating in the liberation of Paris. Pulling back along the entire front, the shattered Germans were forced to re-establish their position in a more defensible location that the Allies would struggle to break through during the remainder of 1944. But the die was cast. It was only a matter of time before the overwhelming resources of the Allies would surmount the retreating Germans, forcing them back across the Rhine River and into the heartland of Germany proper, where in May of 1945 the American and British armies would link up with the Soviets and force the surrender of the now collapsed and defeated 'Thousand-Year Reich'.

The numerous LSTs unloading onto the recently acquired Normandy beaches provided vast quantities of equipment and supplies as the Allied army prepared to march inland. Equipment, supplies and personnel unloading on narrow beach fronts soon led to a serious traffic congestion problem as more arriving material awaited disembarkation.
(US Coast Guard)

The wrecked Mulberry harbour at Omaha Beach after the 'Great Storm' of 19–21 June. This Mulberry was never repaired.
(US Navy)

The American Military Cemetery at Colleville-sur-Mer, overlooking Omaha Beach. The cemetery contains the graves of over 9,000 American soldiers killed during the campaign in France. (RJP)

Heavy equipment, armour and personnel being unloaded onto the recently acquired Normandy beaches via the British Mulberry harbour off Gold Beach, Arromanches, as the Allied army prepared to drive inland. (US Coast Guard)

American soldiers fighting in the difficult French Bocage region. (NARA)

An American M-10 tank destroyer firing on a German position. (US Army)

German soldiers surrendering to American tanks in the French Bocage area. (NARA)

A German soldier killed defending the important port of Cherbourg. Cherbourg, near Utah Beach, was high on the Allies' list of objectives. When finally captured, several weeks after D-Day, the harbour and its facilities had been completely demolished by the surrendering Germans. It would take the rest of the summer to repair. (NARA)

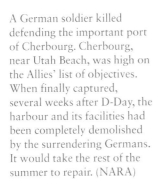

Above: German soldiers put up
stiff resistance behind all five of
the newly taken beaches as the
Allies sought to advance into
the open areas of north-western
France. This German soldier
appears to be armed with the
MG-42 machine gun. (NARA)

Left: General George Patton,
commander of the American
3rd Army. Patton's units swept
around the American right
(western) flank, encircling the
German defenders to trap and
destroy virtually the entire
German force within the
Falaise Pocket. (US Army)

Destroyed German tanks along a French road in the Falaise Pocket. (NARA)

Americans on parade in the newly liberated city of Paris. It was the Normandy invasion, Operation Overlord, that made this achievement possible. (LOC)

Conclusion

In 1940, the narrow and forbidding waters of the English Channel had prevented Hitler from invading Britain. That same moat of water, in 1803–05, had also stymied the armies of Napoleon Bonaparte. But it could not deter the Allies in 1944; nor did it rescue Hitler and the Germans by preventing a successful landing of the combined Allied forces. The Allies had prepared long and carefully as they fashioned overwhelming resources to be projected by a mighty 7,000-ship flotilla, carrying over 150,000 soldiers, while shielded by an invincible air umbrella of over 7,500 airplanes. But more significant was the Allied will: the will to expend the effort, energy, cost and pain of sacrifice on the great cause. The cause went beyond winning a battle. It was an endeavour that was not only strategically necessary to win a war, but truly morally correct and righteous – the elimination of Adolf Hitler and his Third Reich's stranglehold over Europe. Seemingly insurmountable difficulties were overcome at all stages of the Overlord operation: from planning, to staging, to execution. But most significant was the sheer determination to seize 50 miles of French beach held tightly in the grasp of the occupying German Wehrmacht. Beaches that Nazi forces were equally determined to hold at any cost to ensure the ruthless domination of Hitler's Fortress Europe.

Without a doubt, had the D-Day incursion been thrown back into the sea, the course of the war would have been seriously altered. Perhaps the Soviet Red Army would have driven through Germany and into France before the Allies recovered or even managed to attempt a reinvasion. Certainly, had the invasion been just two weeks later, it would have been devastated by the 'Great Storm' of 19–22 June, which caused more damage than was inflicted by the Germans during the invasion, and perhaps preventing a recovery until the spring of 1945. Had the invasion occurred during the week of the storm the entire operation could have been wrecked and the outcome of the war in terms of Germany's defeat and the arrangement of post-war politics and boundaries demonstrably different. Indeed, many things could have occurred to defeat the invasion, but it did prove successful, overcoming all of its flaws, delays and difficulties in preparation and execution. Still to come would be the drive through France at a cost of 125,000 American casualties, and another 85,000 Allied casualties while decimating German defences, with over 250,000 German casualties and over

250,000 captured. The liberation of France would remain bitter and violent. And it would remain for the Western Allies to cross the Rhine River and occupy one-half of Germany, absorbing more frightful casualties and the future confrontation with their former ally, Soviet Russia, ushering in the start of the next forty years of Cold War. The Second World War had not even been concluded before the tremors of the ensuing global split were already being felt, but the reoccupation of France and the liberation of the western half of Europe would be ensured by the dramatic and determined action of D-Day, 6 June 1944.

It had been a struggle; a costly struggle and at times a desperate struggle. Looking back from the comfort of the twenty-first century the success may seem to have been easier than it actually was, but victory was never inevitable. The ultimate truth resides in the courage, stamina and determination of the Allied nations to believe in the moral cause which they honoured. The epitome of this effort was accepting the challenge of re-entering Western Europe through the imagination and implementation of Operation Overlord and the D-Day invasion.

Bibliography

Ambrose, Stephen E., *D-Day: The Climactic Battle* (Simon & Schuster, 1994).

Badsey, Stephen, *Normandy 1944* (Osprey Publishing, 1990).

Balkowski, Joseph, *Omaha Beach: D-Day June 6, 1944* (Stackpole Books, 2004).

Beevor, Anthony, *D-Day: The Battle for Normandy* (Viking Penguin Books, 2009).

Berthon, Simon and Joanna Potts, *Warlords* (Da Capo Press, 2006).

Brinkley, Douglas, and Ronald Drez, *Voices of Valor* (Bullfinch Press, 2004).

Budiansky, Stephen, *Air Power* (Penguin Books, 2004).

Ford, Ken, and Steven Zaloga, *Overlord: The D-Day Landings* (Osprey Publishing, 2009).

Gelb, Norman, *Ike and Monty* (William Morrow, 1994).

Hanson, Victor Davis, *The Second World Wars* (Basic Books, 2017).

Hall, Anthony, *D-Day: Day by Day* (Chartwell Books, 2012).

Jordan, Jonathan, *American Warlords* (Penguin Books, 2015).

Keegan, John, *Six Armies in Normandy* (Penguin Books, 1982).

Messenger, Charles, *The D-Day Atlas* (Thames & Hudson, 2004).

Overy, Richard, *The Bombers and the Bombed* (Penguin Books, 2013).

Penrose, Jane (ed.), *The D-Day Companion* (Osprey Publishing, 2004).

Perry, Mark, *Partners in Command* (Penguin Books, 2007).

Symonds, Craig L., *Neptune* (Oxford University Press, 2014).

Tillman, Barrett, *D-Day Encyclopedia* (Regnery History, 2014).

Van der Vat, Dan, *D-Day: The Greatest Invasion* (Bloomsbury, 2003).

Endnotes

1. Keegan, *Six Armies*, p. 55.
2. Ambrose, *D-Day*, p. 113.
3. Tillman, *D-Day Encyclopedia*, p. 267.
4. Budiansky, *Air Power*, p. 303 or Keegan, *Six Armies*, p. 143.
5. Keegan, *Six Armies*, pp. 60–1.
6. Tillman, *D-Day Encyclopedia*, p. 222.
7. Ambrose, *D-Day*, p. 251.
8. Overy, *The Bombers and the Bombed*, p. 387.
9. Ibid., pp. 390–91.
10. Ibid., p. 391.
11. Ibid., p. 391.
12. Ibid., p. 391.
13. Budiansky, *Air Power*, p. 300.
14. Ibid., pp. 300–2.
15. Ibid., p. 300.
16. Ibid., pp. 302–3.
17. Tilllman, *D-Day Encyclopedia*, p. 4.
18. Beevor, *D-Day*, p. 63 or Penrose, *D-Day Companion*, pp. 175–6.
19. Hall, *D-Day: Day by Day*, p. 169.
20. Keegan, *Six Armies*, p. 76 and Tillman, *D-Day Encyclopedia*, p. 4.
21. Tillman, *D-Day Encyclopedia*, p. 4 or Penrose, *D-Day Companion*, p. 176–7.
22. Ambrose, *D-Day*, p. 201.
23. Ibid., p. 203.
24. Ibid., p. 221.
25. Ibid., p. 222 via Leigh-Mallory.
26. Ibid., pp. 278–9.
27. Ibid., p. 287.

Index